A Path to
Future
Sales Success

How an **individual** with zero sales experience freely
shares how he rose from novice to company sales
leader with forty years of sales **successes**.

John Means, RHU

authorHOUSE®

AuthorHouse™
1663 Liberty Drive
Bloomington, IN 47403
www.authorhouse.com
Phone: 833-262-8899

Published by AuthorHouse 06/22/2022

ISBN: 978-1-6655-6312-3 (sc)
ISBN: 978-1-6655-6310-9 (hc)
ISBN: 978-1-6655-6311-6 (e)

Library of Congress Control Number: 2022911483

Print information available on the last page.

This book is printed on acid-free paper.

Contents

Acknowledgements

Mary Ann for her total support

Tammy a great Christian Author for Advice

Gil and Joyce for their prayers and for being there

Kyle a great illustrator

Lisa and J. R an outstanding IT department

Motivation or Training?

When I first started in the sales profession, with a family to support and no formal sales training I resorted to reading anything I could find on the subject. Back in those days (when Moses was building the Ark) there were only a few books based on selling from actual field experience It was easy to find motivational, and rah-rah books, however, with three children totally depending on me, I did not need motivation; I needed training. By the way, I did say Moses instead of Noah just to make sure you were participating with me.

Many people speak and write about motivation and think this is what one needs to make sales. There is a significant difference between motivation and training. I have attended countless meetings that leave me with the "warm fuzzes" and no direction as to where and when to use these good feelings.

I am sure you have experienced the same feelings. After good motivational speakers we feel that we can charge right out and use positive attitude and the sales will double or triple. However, these "warm fuzzes" immediately begin to fade once the meeting is over. And we return to where we were, and the speakers are long gone presenting in another town with the same results for other salespeople who invest in their systems hoping for more sales and income. Don't get me wrong, there is a definite place for motivation in every salesperson's life. At times we need motivation just to get out there and make the sale.

My thoughts are to use the money you have budgeted for improving sales and advertising to money invested for quality sales training. I am talking about courses that will teach you how to improve your sales not to just get you fired up and ready to go.

What should one do to make more sales? First of all, make your plan.

(See the section "APE). It is my goal in this book to provide you with actual experience from sales over the last 40+ years.

Secondly, make sure that you know the difference between training and motivation. As I have said, you need to have the experiences from others in actual sales and then practice your sales ideas until they become habits for your presentations. I do not believe in "canned talks or presentations" but I do believe in knowing the Listening. specific steps involved in selling. If you know a few specific situations and continue to learn more as you go along the sales road you will find that most situations related to the buying of your product or services can be covered by most ideas you acquire from your constant and devoted, preparation.

Where can one go to learn sales training practices?

1. Surround yourself with positive, successful people. Listen to them.
2. Join your professional trade associations.
3. Join network groups in your community.
4. Read your trade publications.
5. Listen the Sunday sermon or homilies. Here you will find the positive energy you need each week.
6. Read, Read, and Read books and case studies on how to sell.
7. Listening skills are a must. Watch videos about how to really listen. Also really listen to your family and friends when they talk.
8. Visit whenever possible with sales leaders in your office or territories. Everyone has different sales tools and ideas.
9. Attend webinars provided by your company or associations.
10. Become a good storyteller. Related stories equal sales. Clients often like to tell or hear stories related to your subject. Personal experiences are a fascination to everyone.

Examples from the above list

1. Successful people do not focus on the negative. They are always looking for what they need to improve and are usually willing to share what they use in sales. Just listen to them.
2. Trade Associations have training at meetings and webinars. Here you can pick up on new sales tips if you just listen.
3. Network clubs or groups have many people sharing ideas and experiences in sales. Just listen to what they say.
4. Many sales presentations are presented by industry leaders in trade publications. This is a good place to learn new sales tips by listening with your eyes.
5. Sunday Sermons of Homilies often contain sales training in disguise. Instead of nodding off or thinking of other things, Listen for those special stories or sales gems.
6. Books on how to sell are still a great source of sales training. For those who listen to the authors many new tips are provided in their words.
7. When you listen to people, videos, and recordings you gain selling skills.
8. It is good to listen around the office to other people and their stories of that last big sale, or even the last small sale. By accident other salespeople are always sharing sales training.
9. Company webinars are designed by sales professionals to help you make more sales. These work if you are listening, not emailing, getting coffee, dozing, etc.
10. People like to listen to a good story. Make sure it is about your item and how is helps others.

The lists above provide sources for sales training. The best word in sales training is in the list above.

Do you know what it is? Listening!

Everybody Sells

Many sales people often ask what I do to make a sale. It is as if they are looking for a sure thing sales process that works in every interview. Let me tell you there is no such "Magic Pill" that will make the sale for you.

However, there are some steps that will result in your desired result, a Closed Sale. In this chapter it is my desire to share these steps that often help in the sales process. I will be using the term prospective buyer here but later throughout the book I will refer to those people as prospects.

1. It is good to find early common ground. When you first start the interview find the prospect's interest. Don't be the same as every other person in the client's office. Example. I will give you two samples: One prospect had a large sail fish on the office wall, and he often said "I am so tired of everyone asking about that darn fish. The second prospect had an autographed baseball on his desk, his comment was "Does everyone who comes in here have to pick up that ball and ask me about it." So how can you be different from every other salesperson who comes in. Listen to them. For the first one you might say I see you fish then ask if he gets to go out very often. His answer will tell you if he still fishes and what he likes or he might say that he no longer fishes. Either way you did not say the same as all the others. With the baseball, it might be good

to ask if he has a favorite team and how often does he get to a game. Then listen how he directs the conversation's path. Again, you noticed the items like other people but did not just jump to the obvious. Family pictures can often be a good warm starter. But you need to listen. A divorce might have a negative influence. Either way you are on common ground. Don't take a lot of time and do not let the prospect take control of the meeting.

2. Over the last 40+ years the number one thing I have found that helps the most with the sales process is **Participation.** Without the client being involved it is very difficult to create need or get the client to agree. Today there are very few pipe smokers, and I am glad. In the past if you encountered a pipe smoker, they always gave very few signs and could hide behind the pipe. Maybe they were biting so hard on the stem of that pipe thereby hiding their true feelings. Pipe smokers were hard, if not impossible to read. Even one who can hide their emotions, need to be involved with the process. One of the best ways to always involve a prospect is to ask a question. The more questions you use the more you control the process. Keep the client involved and participating. Again, always be listening to the client.

3. Today as in the past there has always been High Pressure salespersons and their tactics. I hope you are not H/P, but if you are don't be offended here, you should try and use these suggestions to your benefit. A true and successful salesperson is an honorable person in an honorable career. Having worked most of my career, in the insurance sales industry I soon learned the fastest way to empty a room is to say your are involved in "multi-level marketing". Which can often be a very high-pressure sales event. The second fastest and almost in a photo finish with MLM is to say you sell insurance. Again, too many unscrupulous people have worked in both. True professional salespeople are **PROFESSIONAL.** What do they do?

- They learn very specific sales skills designed to help their clients.
- They are not amateurs.
- They work in the best interest of their clients. (non-professionals focus only on their interest)
- They learn their product and how to simplify it to their prospects.
- They learn quality sales techniques.
- They observe the actions and questions of their clients.
- They learn the differences in competitors' products. And they work to show how and where their product is superior.
- They constantly study and attend training of specific ways to improve selling.
- They do not dwell on the negatives.
- They have a positive mental attitude.
- They have enough knowledge as to how their product or service will benefit the client.
- They love to tell stories. Especially those related to what they are selling.
- They are always low pressure and relaxed. High pressure only creates tension and most likely the loss of the sale.
- They have empathy. Professionals know that they need to put themselves in the other person's shoes.
- They have enthusiasm.

I stated enthusiasm last because I have a side story here. Years ago, and up to today a great training course used and is using the quote "Act enthusiastic and you will be enthusiastic." The trainer said you needed to animate and include actions in order to create true enthusiasm. Example: You should pound your fist on something to build your enthusiasm.

Here is the story. It was just at the end of lunch hour. I was parked outside the building waiting to go in for the first afternoon interview. While waiting I decided to use the fist pounding approach to build my enthusiasm before the sales meeting. So, sitting in my car I started to pound on the dash of the car. A car came by where I was parked and looked at me pounding. Upon being ushered into my prospect's office I sat down and the client to be, said "Did you get your radio fixed." Yes, he was in the car that passed my pounding. Needless to say, that was the last time I ever used the pounding approach.

4. Most training programs are weak and many times they are produced by people who are not and may never have been in the field. Most trainers want to talk about the "Sales Interview". Today, let's start eliminating the words sales interview from our vocabulary. What should we do? Let's use the term "**Sales Conversation".** Your presentation should be a non-threatening and relaxed <u>conversation</u>. A sales meeting, sales interview, sales pitch, etc. are often adversarial events. In this approach there are always two sides, sometimes one who is nonparticipating. " Sales Conversation" is also two sided but it is cordial and socially interactive. When you have an interview with a prospect make it a sales conversation.

During the conversation be sure to <u>listen to the client.</u>
Remember everybody sells! And your first sale should be to sell yourself.

Be on the lookout

Throughout this book we are emphasizing one major theme for sales. I hope you have found it, but if not stay with us and you will find it soon.

Here we are going to focus on an important part of that theme. Buying signals and non-verbal communication from your prospect that turn them into a customer. Through countless hours of client focused body language seminars, training courses, and lots of research about the signs of prospects that shows they agree and are ready to buy. We naturally pay attention to body language around us every day. Knowing how to read body language and making the appropriate response to it will be one of the greatest weapons in one's sales arsenal.

Prospect buying signals are important in the sales process, but they are only half the story. In a sales presentation the presenter's body language is just as important. So, lets' jump in starting with prospect signals and learn how to use those signals to our advantage. Remember, you should actively engaged with the client to "hear" their body language, while you are listening to the actual words they are saying

Customer reactions

Body language is important in a sales interview because it affects how customers are reacting to what you are showing and saying to them.

I have never been one to use anything scripted or filled with data in the sales interview, but knowing data and information is critical for the salesperson. Here is some good information to know.

In a recent UCLA study, researchers learned:

- 7% of actual communication is based on the words said
- 38% is based on the tone and inflection of the voice
- 55% of the balance comes from body language

With 55% of our communication based on body language we must certainly devote time to the development of the specific skills to make this important factor work in our favor. How can we do that and what do we look for?

Top performing salespeople are generally high in emotional intelligence. They have the ability to listen, observe, and know the unspoken signals in our communications.

Therefore, we need to delve into some of the basic signs and signals that our prospects emit during the sales interview. First let's look at the **negative signals.**

- Crossed arms (and sometimes crossed legs) are an indication that the prospect is resisting your proposal.
- Smiles can be a deception. Often an insincere smile hides a negative feeling about what the prospect is thinking. A true smile causes the crow's feet to appear around the eyes. No crow's feet = no agreement.
- Covering the mouth is a negative buying signal. If the person in the interview places a finger or hand over their mouth it is not the time to close.
- Relaxing in a chair and looking around the areas indicates they are bored and not interested.
- "Look me in the eye" is often considered to indicate truthfulness. Watch out for the person who is making an extra effort to stare into your eyes, they may be lying.
- A clinched fist indicates a firm resistance. Time to cut the tension.

- Excessive nodding indicates anxiety about your presentation. Normal nodding is good but in excess it indicates you need to ease their feelings.
- Frowning or raising of the eyebrows also indicates distrust or disbelief in the information.

These are not all the negative body images and buying signals but should give you a good start of developing your skills of listening, observing, and addressing the immediate situation. I want you to remember that **THESE BUYING SIGNALS USUALLY ARE SUDDEN AND ARE AN UNCONCIOUS REACTION.**

Now let's take an in-depth examination of the **Positive Images** of body language and buying signals.

In this area we will focus on the things displayed by a prospect that indicate a positive reaction and possibly the time to close the sale.

Eyes... the windows into the mind.

- Eyes can be a negative sign but are very positive signals. Let's look at the pupils. We have just a few areas of the body over which we have no control. If you notice pupils narrowing the client is telling that they have concerns with what you are saying.
- If a prospect is looking at you it tells you that they are thinking about what you are presenting.
- Looking at the paperwork or materials related to the presentation they are focusing on the materials rather than listening to you. I have learned over the span of my career that it is best not to provide materials at the beginning of your presentation. Like I stated earlier I do not like to use data and complicated charts etc. in the presentation. To me concept selling (more later) is the successful salesperson's main goal.
- If the client's eyes move to another area of the room that is okay, as long as the eyes quickly return their focus to your presentation. If the eyes focus on the door, it says the

prospect is bored and wanting to leave. This is a good time for questions to the person.

In summary on the eyes, you want the prospective buyer (hereinafter referred to as the prospect) to focus on you with eye contact. Constant staring you down is showing their intimidation for you or the product. What you want the prospect to do is make eye contact with you 60% to 70% of the time.

Hands …. the second highest form of communication.

- Patting the hand or drumming fingers on the table shows that the prospect is impatient with your presentation. Here you should ask a question to refocus, but most of all speed up your work. People who are not analytical often become frustrated with facts and figures. They only want the key information and move on. On the other hand, the analytical personality is really wanting all the details. As an example, engineers are often very focused on details. Coaches often only want the basics and move on.
- If things on the table are getting attention there is an indication of boredom or annoyance with you. Watch for playing with paper clips, paperwork, or a pen or pencil.
- Leaning on an armrest with their hands in your direction is a sign that their subconscious is telling that they are done and want to end the meeting.
- Pointing fingers is another sign of intimidation from the prospect.

Feet … a surprise in sales.

- Earlier in the negative signs area we discussed the crossed feet as a negative. Feet can also indicate positive. Most people have worked on facial expressions to prevent salespeople from knowing their feelings, but they pay little or no attention to their feet.

- When working with ladies they often have their legs crossed. This may not be a negative or a positive sign.
- Positive feelings for something are displayed by having the feet pointing toward the presenter. If they are pointing away from the presenter negative feelings are indicated.
- Bouncing their knees by basic jiggling usually indicates that the person is not interested. Here a question of relaxing statement can bring them back. Here it is important that you can determine why they are not responding positively. And turn them around immediately.

Facial features ... always working from birth to death.

- One of the first things we learn is smiling. A smile is always welcomed. (well maybe not at certain times at a funeral) A smile is a very productive way to get a positive response.
- Smiling and nodding at the same time is a great indicator that you are on the right track. Keep running the train.
- At times it is time to change the direction of your presentation. One of these is if you see stress on the face. i.e., wrinkling of the nose, a frown, narrowing of the eyes, a stiff jaw, or tightening of the lips. Here is where questions can help you discover their concerns.

Most Successful Buying Signs

It is important to know the signs of acceptance and rejection. However, if you are having a hard time remembering our discussion on these pages here are simple things to watch for. I call these my Late Night Top Ten List.

- Suddenly touching the contract, brochure, or application.
- Interrupting with a specific detail question.
- Leaning forward to see or hear details
- Opening a clinched fist.
- Touching the nose says more information.
- Covering the mouth says "I don't believe that".

- Offering refreshment or a drink. (best to thank them and say you would like to finish and then we can enjoy the offered item)
- A twinkle in the eyes.
- Relaxing. Suddenly just a simple sigh or lay back motion.

Below is the **#1** of my top ten list!

Suddenly Touching One's Chin

I cannot guarantee that this will always work for you, but it has never failed when I have noticed the sudden touching of the chin.

In Summary

Body language and Buying signals are as important as what is actually being said. A buying signal is not just some gimmick to quickly close and make a fast buck it is just a tool to help the salesperson be closer with the client and recognize how to bind with them. Remember our goal is to form a relationship not a quick sale. This is done by caring and being empathetic with them.

Body language interpretation is just another aspect of being a good listener!

The bottom line is that even if you can't read a person's exact thoughts, you can learn a lot from their body language, and that's especially true when words and body language don't match.

More To Look For

Previously we talked about some of the most important body language and buying signals. Those signals were important and usually happen suddenly. You need to constantly be on the lookout because they come so quickly.

There are other interest showing signs and signals we need to be aware of when making our presentations. Many times, these events are not sudden, but may be very subtle in their appearance. It is not hard to identify them, but you should be aware of human nature, behavioral science and some psychology. There are lots of courses on these subjects online and in your library.

Sales people with lots of experience will tell you to use your common sense and as the old railroad signs told us; Stop, Look, and Listen.

Pay attention and always be ready to identify any of these signals.

- Questions – it is not bad news if your prospect is asking questions during your presentation. If your prospect is listening, questioning, and maybe writing down information; these are great signals of interest. Always make your presentations flexible and have the ability to stop when needed. At the beginning of my sales presentations I always say, don't hesitate to stop me and ask your questions. I do not think it is a good idea to make them wait for the end of a presentation for their questions.

- Heads you win – Watch your prospects' head movements. If they are nodding during your presentation, interest is indicated.

- Not in person, no problem - Listen closely for pauses, no questions, and a feeling of distractions. Use a question or pause to get the prospect back in focus on your presentation. Here is an example: I am often guilty of when talking with a person on the phone. If I am at my desk the computer screen becomes a distraction. I find myself hesitating, not listening, and failing to answer questions. Sometimes my wife will remind me to pay attention when she wants to talk. Even in person I still am easily distracted. Listen closely to your prospects for signs that you are not paying close attention.

- What is needed here – do they have a problem? If they tell you about a problem that you can help with, they are telling you they need more information and are definitely interested. We as sales people tend to try to discover the problem during our presentation. Many times, the "real problem" does not come out early. If the prospect voluntarily offers information on their real situation, you are well on the way to a touchdown.

- What about Joe with XTZ Corp. - If your prospect offers information on their current rep or his company, they are telling you they are shopping for a better solution to their needs. As I have said many times before in this book, build lasting relationships. Many times, people only see the sales person when the sale is made. Spend time and stay in touch after the sale. Example: Joe, gets the sale. He is happy with the commission and moves on to the next prospect. Once the sale is complete he forgets about the long term relationship development. This rep will possibly make a good income for a little while. But without long term relationships they will fail. Long term clients make a career while wham bam sales make a job. Jobs become boring.

- Eye Contact – Who needs to make eye contact? Both the rep and the prospect. Yes, the eyes do not lie. Their contact means interest. Your eye contact indicates the same in their direction. Your contact shows that you have interest in them. If for some reason it is not comfortable to make eye contact you can look directly at their nose and it will appear as eye contact. Mainly you must be interested and interesting.

- Let's do lunch – Meeting again later can be a slippery slope that we need to trod cautiously. Sometimes this is a quick way to leave a situation, especially if it is brought up by the client. Watch closely. If you bring up meeting again and the client agrees to meet later it is a positive indication of strong interest. As a reminder, set the appointment right then. With today's electronic calendars and appointment books it is easy to schedule on the spot.

Not all signals are positive. There are signs that produce identifiable negative signals. Watch for these indications that your prospect is not interested

- Not interested – There are times when the client is not interested and will just tell you that. Most people try to use the softest method of telling someone no, saying something like, this is really nice but maybe later. But if they come outright and say I am not interested, that is your signal that they truly do not want your product or service. Don't take it personal or as a challenge to keep trying. This is the time to thank them for their time and say goodbye as a gracious professional.

- Do not have time – some prospects are reluctant to schedule a meeting time with you in the beginning. This can be an early indication of lack of interest in what you have. Not being interested may be a matter of timing. Sometimes it may be better to not press for an appointment and try again later. Thank the prospect and offer to contact them later. Stay positive, and follow up as you promised.

- No budget – many times a person will not be willing to share the budget information their company has for your type of purchases. They may not have a budget or they just do not want to share it. This can be an indicator of lack of interest, but do not give up on a presentation. It is often good to show how your product can improve the bottom line. They may be conservative and only interested in their financial gain. It could be that a tight budget is the problem. Here if they are trying close the door on you, they may be opening a window. At this point if you discover tight dollars move your focus to the window opening and show how how your item can save them.
- Who? – I have often found that the person to whom you are speaking may not be the one who actually can make the decision you need. Early on it is best to make sure the person you are talking to can make the call. This may take extra questions and probing. Don't waste your time with someone not in control. A good probing question might be, " If we can find the right item for your company, would you be able to make the final decision or does it need to go a committee or another area of the company?"
- Other options – the prospect may show no current interest by indicating they are still researching providers, products, or checking to make sure they are selecting the best solution for them. Sometimes here there are indications they could be looking for a better deal. This does not mean they will not go with you, so keep probing to discover the true meaning.
- Most sales trainers stress the importance of the thank you note or letter following a sale. But what about the no-sale interview? It is always good to send something thanking them for their time and that you enjoyed visiting with them. Remind them that you are still willing to work with them in the future. By the way, this is a good time to enclose a couple of your cards. Why two? They may give one to a subordinate or an assistant, keep one for their file or throw

them both in the trash. As I said earlier business cards are cheap. Enough said? It is also good to make a follow up call in six months just to ask if there is anything you can do for them. Electronic devices have a myriad of ways to remind you when to call. I have at times called every six months for two years. Yes, sometimes I did end up with a sale. Don't give up too early.

- Persistence – many times it is necessary for a sales person to keep trying after a negative signal. A hero of mine is Wyllie Coyote. Talk about persistent, he never stops trying to get the road runner. He always gets up and tries again. You too need to be like Wyllie. Keep trying, Keep trying, Keep trying.

Here is one of my" keep trying" side stories. When my wife and I were first married we were still in college. But soon were going to need a place to live. I discovered a mobile home for sale. The seller was moving across country and it would cost more to transport the trailer than it would be worth. He wanted $1000 dollars and take over his payments. I of course told him I did not have a thousand dollars, but I would be happy to take over the loan. He refused! Every day after school I knocked on his door. "Have you sold the home yet?" I did this every day for 30 days straight. It was nearing time for his move and he needed to make his decision. He finally said okay, we lived in the trailer for three years and paid off the loan. Persistency did and does pay off.

Most all sales trainers and training programs feature the "Buying Signals" that give positive information to the person trying to make the sale. It appears to be that the prospect is the only one emitting these signs.

What about the presenter? Does he or she not give signs that the prospect can also see from the salesperson? Here I give a most resounding YES. I would like to give some background information and then we will delve into the actual signs we give.

Relationships

One of the most significant things in this area is that successful people attract successful people. You should try this experiment for yourself.

The next time you enter a room of people, be it a party, club meeting, sales meeting, or any other place where people gather. Yes, this even includes church. Look around the room where people are milling around or having conversations. You can pick out the successful people by noticing who has formed groups. Those with "negative" or unsuccessful patterns will be gathered together in one area and those with "successful" patterns will be in another area. I have found that about 90% of the time you will find this to be true. The next time you are watching a movie look closely and the "Good Guy" will always be associating with the winners. This holds true in real life and entertainment venues.

Over the years during the times that I was in a slump, or my attitude was down I discovered that sales were down I was not connecting with my successful peer group. I have always wanted to have people around that have a winning mindset. This would bring me back.

Attitude

I have always said I would rather have five pounds of attitude over ten pounds of Aptitude.

Over the years many "good salespeople, (you know the ones who score at the top of those written ability test) have failed dramatically in the actual sales field. Here are the excuses.

24

- Poor management
- Lack of competitive products
- Not enough sales training
- No encouragement
- Not enough quality leads
- Company did not advertise enough
- The strength of the company was weak

Yes, I said these were excuses. Having been in management and field sales at the same time I have heard the excuses and even felt that I too was failing because of one or more of these. This was the situation that causes us to lie to ourselves and in a management role it causes the sales manager and the salesperson to lie to one another. There is a positive way to eliminate these as I discovered early in my career. With my time management system an individual and/or managers can no longer kid each other and stay on track to sales. (See the chapter on the APE)

Motivation comes from within and not from outside sources. Seminar after seminar over the years has stressed that their methods and training can bring about the necessary motivation for success. One of my favorite motivational authors and speaker is the late Zig Ziglar. I could attend one of his presentations and become so "fired up" that I could not wait to get back in the field. True Zig was pure energy and instilled the desire to succeed. I was even fortunate to have breakfast with Zig before a seminar and no one could have been higher. But even with the great Zig the enthusiasm would soon fade. But even with the motivated plan and a return to the field it soon gets difficult again.

As Mike Tyson said, "Everyone has a plan until you get punched in the face". Rejection punches us in the face.

Keeping the attitude positive and the motivation on a high level can be achieved. Here a few things you can do to help keep things going your way toward the success you desire.

- Remember a true salesperson knows that they are there to help the consumer.

- Forget commissions. No matter how bad you need a sale keep the client first. Take care of the client and the commissions will take care of themselves.
- Keep a $100 bill in your pocket. Yes, attitude can improve when you know you have that c-note.
- Listen to your manager. Most likely he or she has been in the same spot and can help. Never fear to ask for help.
- Don't focus on the news. Most of the time the news media can provide us with excuses not to be motivated with a good attitude.
- Love your family. Nothing motivates like that smile from your spouse or that little one who has only total love without equivocation.
- Count your blessings every day. Remember, the opportunity we have as salespersons is like the "money tree" just go in the field and pick what you need.

Appearance

You do not have to have the most expensive clothes, but your attire should be neat and pressed. The next time you are In a restaurant look at the servers. One is neat and one is a wrinkled mess. Which one would you want to wait on you? Be truthful here. Also if you can see the tips on the table which do you thing gets the most money for their service?

Now I would like to share a story of how little things can help your sales.

Very early in my career I was fortunate to meet one of the biggest characters in the insurance sales industry. I will refer to him as R.A. from Virginia. When I first met R. he was wearing Jeans with holes in them (before this was the style) well-worn running shoes, and a polyester shirt. He was "off duty" and this is what he wore then.

When he was at work his apparel completely changed. He referred to his clothes as his work uniform. It consisted of two Hickey-Freeman custom suits. Three Countess Mara ties (very expensive for the day) and two pairs of Florsheim Royal Imperial Shoes. His suits had six custom made inside pockets. These pockets were used to carry his brochures and all other sales needs. R. always said if you carry a brief case, you might as well make a sign for your chest that says salesperson.

I told you this story of how a very limited wardrobe can help you with your appearance that will make sales. A good appearance can also really improve your attitude. By the way R. and I both worked for the same company and while I was the leading life salesperson, he led the company in disability sales.

For many years I had R.'s same uniform. As I write this chapter, I am wearing jeans and a sweatshirt.

Listening and Honesty

Learning the skill to be a good listener is imperative to being successful in sales. First, always **BE HONEST!**

In sales as in life," Honesty is the best policy". Here, I have established my basis for honesty in sales. Before completing any sales I ask myself if this three legged- stool will stand.

1. **IS IT GOOD FOR THE CLIENT?**
2. **IS IT GOOD FOR THE SALESPERSON?**
3. **IS IT GOOD FOR THE COMPANY?**

I don't know if you have ever had the pleasure of milking a cow or not. But if one leg of the three-legged stool breaks while milking down you go. It is the same in sales if any part of the three questions above is NO, down you go.

Secondly, learn to listen. At times in an interview, I tend to forget that even though I know my material and have heard it a thousand times, this is the first the time the customer has heard it. It is easy to ramble on trying to get to the end of the presentation that we forget the client. If they do not ask questions, make sure you pause and ask if they have any questions. If they are asking questions, it is a good sign of interest. Always remember, Client First.

When you have time ask your child, grandchild, or any little one to tell you their favorite story. This even works with teenagers. You will be amazed how this improves your skills. How about really listening to your spouse. And here is a good one, listen to the gas station attendant and his story. How about going to another part of the country and listen to the accents they have. It can be amazing and really help. Listen to everyone...they all have a story to tell.

YES...

In our sales conversations what are we looking for? What is it that gets adrenalin flowing? What is the magic word to our ears? What is it that gives the salesperson the high that only salespeople know? What drives selling?

YES!

We are constantly asked what do you use for closing. Most trained people in the field are always looking for the magic word or phrase that will "close the sale".

Well guess what, gang. I have no Idea.

However, I do have some things that might help you close more sales and at the end of this chapter I will share my <u>one</u> closing that has worked for over 40 years of selling.

Traditional closing Ideas that may help:

- The Puppy Dog Close – This is a very traditional close that probably has been used on you and maybe without your even knowing it. One of the best users of the Puppy Dog is a car salesperson. Did you ever notice the good salesperson wants to get you behind the wheel for a "test drive"? Sure, here they are getting you to at least pet the puppy See how soft and new it feels. Great sales people go one step further, they make arrangements for you to drive the car home. They may say to see if it fits in your garage, let the rest of your family see it, or simply take time to really test it out. This is classic puppy dog. They want you to take the car home. As you drive down the street, the neighbors are noticing you, your friends are seeing you with "your" new car. Yes, you are a victim. Now it would be to embarrassing to return it after that. You can even close with the puppy dog on an intangible sale. There is a three day right to resend the decision on an in-home sale. In insurance there is a "free look" provision to change your mind. Even after the policy is issued one usually has thirty days to send it back for a full refund.

Side story here:

One night on having a sales conversation I discovered an individual who needed life insurance to protect his family. His wife wanted him to Purchase it because they needed it. He kept saying he just wanted to think about it overnight. P/D close came to mind. I said," How about this, lets complete the application and your check, keep it while you think and if you change your mind in the morning and I will return everything to you. The advantage for you is that you can have coverage while thinking. He finally agreed and applied. The next morning, I received a call not from him but from his wife. He was hit by a drunk driver and killed as he was going to his night shift job. Yes, it is a true story and the family received $100,000 of much needed funding. Thanks Puppy Dog from both of us.

- The Insignificant Item Close – here is an idea that has worked for many years. Again, I go to a car salesperson. This is the story of a leading sales rep at a luxury car dealership. He would show a top-of-the-line car and when it was time he said, "Would you like your monogram in silver or gold?" Here he had the prospect make an $80,000 decision on picking a $15 monogramming. This can also be done on a clothing purchase. "Which color (tie, scarf. Etc. do you think goes with this suit. All of these are minor point closes.

On an intangible item use "How would be the best way for you to pay for this." Many times, on this pay question the client will ask "How do you pay?" I have found that for an annual payment I do not say "most people pay this by the year." (that's what everyone else has said) I say, and it is very successful "Annual is Customary" This is a soft way to refer to the payment. Other insignificant closes, without elaboration are: Start each of these by saying *"In your Opinion"*

which would be better blue or silver?
is today's price alright?
and if you were to decide sometime in the future
which one would best suit your needs?
would this fit your needs.
is the price comfortable for you?
does this feel good and comfortable?
could we lock in the offer so you could move in
next week?
would it be a good idea for me to hold it for you?

Remember when you ask "in your opinion" you are not asking for a hard decision but rather just a thought to see the direction they are leaning. Here you might just get the decision you are wanting.

It is not knowing a specific closing line, as many trainers suggest, but rather knowing *when* to close. When should you ask for the sale?

When buying signals say he or she has already bought!

Questions, Questions, Questions are the most effective way to learn when it is time to close. I have often had times that I asked for an opinion and had the client say, "actually I think I need it now." You just never know unless you ask. Don't always ask for a decision but getting their frame of mind will guide you to the closing.

- Sales Emotions - the actual close is the result of an emotion rather than the facts presented. Those emotions can be emotional to somewhat vivid. Relaxing is the most convincing reaction to the actual purchase from you. Strong negative emotions indicate more information is needed and a good story can often relax the situation. I use some humor when needed.
- One thing I want you to learn more than anything in this area is:

"FACTS DON'T SELL.....STORIES DO!

- **60,20, 20** - What in the world is this? Here are some facts that might help with your closing. We as salespeople needs to know when to close and not a "canned line" to help us fail to close. Remember this, body language is 60% of all communication, and 20% is by vocal inflection. Well, guess what, that means only 20% comes from what we say. So, if you are looking for a magic bullet phrase on line to make the close, watch for body language, or changes in voice. (Buying signals) You might want to review our buying signal chapter to make sure you know how to identify them for sure. If we rely on what is said for our clues don't forget to recognize Vocal Signals. Some of these statements of questions are:

> How much is this?
> Looks good to me.
> Is this guaranteed?
> I like red.
> What are the sizes again?
> You know I like this better than....

These are only a few of the questions the prospect may use verbally. But remember as we have discussed the sales conversations, we always emphasized for you to use questions in your process. Please do not forget the importance of client questions in the sales conversations.

Also do not forget the obvious:

> I'll take it.
> Where do I sign?
> Do you take credit cards?
> When can you deliver?
> Is this the latest or newest model or program?
> What is the warranty?
> Can I purchase an extended warranty?
> How long does this last?

Poor salespeople base the presentation on memorized presentations and tend to constantly keep on their track. They have been trained to simply move to the close and then close, close, close.

Good salespeople tend to use a guided presentation that provide lots of facts for the prospect. They do rely on specific closes they have learned from their experiences.

Great salespeople are flexible, they put the clients first all the time, are very knowledgeable about their product or service, and they use stories to simplify the information being presented. They are always following our guideline. of constantly listening. The sales world requires you to always be on the alert

Early in this chapter I told you that I would give you my only close that has proven to work for me. I know it is good to have a knowledge of the options of the tried-and-true different closes used over the centuries on closing the sale. I too know of these suggestions as to how to close the sale. Some I have used over the years, but I still rely on one major question for my close.

Here it is.

What do you think about this?

After asking this question, I just shut up. Wait for their comment. Here they will tell you just what they think. Be patient do not speak first. Remember once you ask this question the one who speaks will be the one who completes the sale. If it is the client, they will be conceding and you will have the sale. If you speak first the sale is gone. JUST WAIT AND **LISTEN.**

This question has closed most of my sales over my career and I am sure that it will close for you.

Always be listening.

Prospectors Find Gold

Over the centuries there have been many "gold rushes". People have prospected, fought over, and worked claims trying to find great riches. Yes, the first item listed in the path to "sales riches" is prospecting. In my office I have pictures of prospectors, sayings about prospectors and figurines of prospectors. I know I have been dwelling a lot here about prospecting, but it is the truest way to have continuous sales and rewards in the sales business.

No matter what you are selling, you must continually find new people to talk to. Have you ever noticed when people find a "good deal" they are prone to tell everyone about how great the item or service has been for them? Once you have a satisfied customer, it is easy to get them to help you. Unless you are asking them to help their competitors. Of course, they will not usually want to share their secrets with their direct competition. Here it is good to work on getting prospects that are not in direct competition with them.

Many salespeople have asked me, "How do you find leads?" Everyone seems to be looking for the magic bullet that fits every situation. Sorry Charlie, there is no one simple way to find leads. Believe me I have tried many lead generating methods over the forty + years of successful selling. There is a huge boneyard of attempts that have failed, and only a few good ways to find quality sales opportunities.

Recently I was fortunate to meet with a gentleman who ran a top-rated lead mailing company. In talking with him he explained that he should be the absolute last resort in the as a source for of getting leads. I asked him what he meant, being in the business of selling leads and not encouraging people to use his service. And this came directly from a lead generating sales organization it seemed counterproductive. His explanation was that mailing leads are a lot like cold calls. Mainly they generate a name and number from a responder. Any salesperson first of all should exhaust all other avenues of securing places to find quality prospects. I was very impressed with his honesty and willingness to help people before profit. He advised that before people use his service they should work referrals', personal contacts, and third-party influences. If they still needed prospect leads after all other methods of contact had failed, then use a mailing service. I know many of you feel that mailings are a great source of leads. If so, then by all means, continue to do what you are doing. "If it aint broke don't fix it." But constant work in all prospecting areas may prove to be even better results for you. While talking about mail service leads, I have a good story. Early in my management career, I worked for a company that provided mail return leads to sales reps. These leads came in on a computer run and our job was to put the information on a "lead card" and distribute them weekly to our staff. Generally, the leads came in on Friday and we gave them out at the Monday morning sales meeting. (Much more about weekly meetings in a later chapter.) One Friday no leads arrived. Panic! What would we do for agents who were depending on leads we did not have? Yes, salespeople who use leads become very dependent on them. I thought about it for a while and decided to have my assistant make up some lead cards for them. She simply went through some small-town phone directories and made up some cards that looked exactly like they did every week. Guess What, we had the best week of sales that week. We simply told them these were the freshest leads we had received in a long time. They were fresh for sure. Attitude means everything in sales.

Another way to prospect is to use third party influence. Many times, I worked with organizations and when I could get the club, fraternity, church group, or any other type of organization to recommend my service and products the leads were excellent. Here I used these groups to do the mailings for me. (I covered expenses) These were letters that as I mentioned earlier were sent first class and came from the leader of the organization. When you can get a respected individual in a group to make the contacts, people want to learn about what it is that the group is "endorsing". Yes, it is not an actual endorsement, but it could be, people's perception is that the group is behind me or my product. Recently while working with a church group, I received an invitation to speak at their monthly meeting. I asked about how many people would usually attend and he said about twenty-five. His letter was well written and his description of our service and products that people began talking about the upcoming meeting. On the day of the meeting, I had refreshments for 30 thinking this would be an adequate number for a group of 25. On the day of the meeting, seventy-three members arrived. Quick, door dashed another 45 refreshments. The result was 51 leads, 48 appointments, and 28 sales, and an invitation to next years meeting. To say the least I was amazed at the results. While completing these sales I discovered that the group leader was one of the most influential members of the church and his word was gold. Now you know, his influence was my greatest asset. Third parties can make or break your efforts for leads. It may take some time to get the influence of third parties but take the time and cultivate them. When you gain their confidence, and they see the value you provide they generally want to help you and their group at the same time. Do not rush when starting to work with them. Planning far enough ahead can give you the time you need for third party influence. Finally, third party leads can be the most effective way to gain quality leads. If you will professionally represent yourself, your company, and your products people will be happy to meet and do business with you. Do what you say you will do and never embarrass the leader who is your center of influence.

Here is a question for you. Could this have, been you? After the sale is closed many salespeople tend to want to get out of the appointment as quickly as possible. You know, before the client has time to change their mind. We all fear buyers' remorse and do not want to lose the sale we just made. If you are asking for referrals this does make more credibility for you and cements the just made sale even more. Truthfully, I would venture the speculation that at some point you have just wanted to get out of Dodge as fast as you can. Don't grab and run.

As I ask for referrals, I start with the shoe store story. I tell them that I am like the person who owns the local shoe store, explaining that once a person buys a pair of shoes the owner must replace the stock, and purchase more shoes. If the replacement is not made the store will soon close due to lack of inventory. I am the same way, if I do not replace my stock, I will also go out of business. What is my stock? I need a reserve of people to see. Now you have changed from a future client to a client. So, I have lost some of my stock when you moved from a prospect to an actual client. Therefore, I need your help. Then I go directly to my referral card system below. IT REALLY WORKS!

How? Read on.

Prospect generation does not have to be sophisticated or expensive to get the desired results. A few years ago, we developed a lead generation system that is so simple and cost effective that I was sure it would not work. Most lead generation programs use expensive four color, hard stock mailing pieces. These always look very professional and can attract attention. Many salespeople rely of these methods which is fine, but expensive. Also, these "professional" pieces often look like all the others they receive every week. It is easy to get lost in the crowd. I find that informal personal methods work best for me. From these high impact pieces, they are usually happy with a two to five percent return. So, it takes a lot of pieces made to get sufficient leads. Good for the printers and the ad companies but, expensive for the rep. I guess you are wondering if am negative on this type of contacting prospects What do I do and recommend? Here is what I developed. A referral system that uses new clients to contact those in their circle of influence. How does it work? Let's jump in and see how it works.

Here we will spend some time explaining exactly what you need to do to make this work. Believe me, if you learn these exact steps, you will have a constant flow of new people to see.

1. Have the cards (shown at the end of this chapter) printed on post card stock and the size of a post card. Here I would suggest that you order a large quantity of cards. You will need a lot of them as you use this tested and true system.
2. Clip or rubber band the cards in packs of 5. You may use three if you are not comfortable with five in the early stage of this system. As you continue to use them, five will become an easy and reliable number of requests of your clients.
3. Once the sale is made tell the client you need their help. Start with the "shoe store story". Ask the new client if they would be willing to help you restock your store. Most people are usually inclined to help someone who asks for their help.
4. Bring out your cards. Ask for them to think of a few friends, neighbors, or family members that might benefit from my service. If they are confident, they have made a good deal they like to tell others about their success.
5. Present the cards with the message side up. Here the only put in the new prospects name and they sign on the sincerely line. Turn the cards over.
6. Ask your client if they would mind addressing the post cards for you. (important in their handwriting) If they are having trouble suggest family members, business associates, association members. Anyone with whom they have reactions.
7. Once the card has been completed and addressed, take the back and thank them for helping you and assure them that their friends will be treated just like they were treated.
8. After leaving the sales appointment take the cards to your office and where the stamp will be placed, I like to put

R-name, This reminds me of who gave me the referral. Also, in the spot the stamp covers put the date received.

9. Wait a couple of days, for mailing the cards. It is best not to be too eager to your client. Make a log of whom were mailed cards and the date mailed.

10. Two to three days after mailing make a call to the new prospect. Ask the following question exactly as stated below:
   "Did you receive (referring clients name   ) card? Remember it is the client's card not yours.

11. At this point most prospects will say What is this about.? Tell them that _____ thought you might like the idea I shared with them and felt they wanted them to know about the idea.

12. Ask for the appointment. If they object to scheduling a meeting explain that you are only going to present new information about their needs. And you want to make sure they have the latest information about what you are presenting. If you are making a two call presentation tell them there will not be and sales made at this informational meeting and it will only last a maximum of 17 minutes unless they have questions. I use 17 minutes because everyone else says 15 minutes. When I get to the appointment, I put my watch on their desk and say this is to remind me to stop in 17 minutes. It is up to you to give enough information that questions on their part will arise. Stick with you promise.

13. Schedule the second appointment and be ready to make a sales presentation at that one. Remember, the more time spent with them and the more you educate them,the more your chances of getting a new client and not just a sale.

14. Once they are a client repeat the referral card system with them. If they are happy there is usually little objections to helping you with more contacts.

15. Should you not be able to get an appointment, ask them to call their referring friend and tell them to ask them about

how you helped them with your idea or service. Thank them and tell them will call them later.

You will not get an appointment every time but remember with the low cost of this system you don't need many sales to be in the positive profitability mode. Even if you get only one or two appointments from your center of influence referrals think of how many more sales are out there. Don't ever give up on referrals.

By using the card system and distributing an abundance of business the calls from prospects will come. Both are more effective and less expensive ways to get people to see.

Sales people that I know personally who have used these systems and have mastered their techniques of asking for referrals, today they are not in need of prospects.

Following are some samples of referral cards for various ty pes of sales. If you need to feel welcome to make specific changes that apply to your field. However, I would recommend that you keep the basic format in place.

Also do not print the titles in parentheses on the cards!

John Means, RHU

(PERSONAL FINANACIAL PLANNING)

Dear_____

This will introduce_____
I have recommended that he familiarize you with
A very beneficial program that could benefit you.
Needless to say, you are not obligated in any way.
However, I have personally taken advantage of his
service and feel that you should know about it. If
you are interested please call him at _____

Sincerely_____

(INSURANCE)

Dear_____

This will introduce _____
I have recommended that he familiarize you with
the 2022 benefit changes, that effect you.
Needless to say, you are not obligated in any way.
However, I have personally taken advantage of his
service and feel that you should know about it. If
you want to be assured you have the best coverage and benefits
currently available often at a lower cost.

Sincerely_____

44

(NEW PRODUCT LINE)

Dear_____

This will introduce _____
I have recommended that he familiarize you with
the new 2022 product line and how it benefits you.
Needless to say, you are not obligated in any way.
However, I have personally taken advantage of his service and
feel that you should know about it. I have asked
him to call you in the next couple of days

Sincerely_____

(NEW CAR INFORMATION)

Dear_____

This will introduce _____
I have recommended that he familiarize you with some of the
new advanced automobile electronics and safety features.
Needless to say, you are not obligated in any way.
However, I have personally taken advantage of his
service and feel that you should know about it. I have
asked him to call him in the next few days.

Sincerely_____

(PRE-OWNED CAR)

Dear_____

This will introduce _____
I have recommended that he call you about the value of your
car. You may be able to upgrade your vehicle without changing
your cash flow and at the same time improve your safety.
Needless to say, you are not obligated in any way.
However, I have personally taken advantage of his
service and feel that you should know about it. I have asked him
to call you in the next few days.

Sincerely_____

(GENERAL SALES)

Dear_____

This will introduce _____
I have discovered a very knowledgeable person who puts
clients first and works to find what most benefits you.
Needless to say, you are not obligated in any way.
However, I have personally taken advantage of his
service and feel that you should know about it. I have asked him
to give you a call in the next few days.

Sincerely_____

Remember the basics of having the new client address and sign the
cards. So, when you call you can ask if they received "THEIR "card.
The more you can use a friend or associate's influence the better.

Happy staying busy.

Business Cards are Cheap

Why would I title a chapter "Business Cards are Cheap"? Because it is true. They cost very little and can go along way in advertising. Use them as handouts, recruiting pieces, referrals, pin ups, and leave behinds. Business cards can be one of your most effective marketing items. Let's take a look at the definition and ways to use cards stated above.

- Handouts – this is a system of sharing your cards in mass. Carry business cards with you at all times. I hand them out to people I meet and have people hand them out to their friends and family.
- Recruiting Pieces – You do not have to have one specific card that you use for all purposes. In this case one size does not fit all. You should have cards that point out the purpose for which they are being used . (More later about this when I discuss card designs)
- Referrals – This is the most economically, efficient way to use your card for leads and future appointments. (Again, there will be more to come later)
- Pin ups – no not super hunks, or bathing suit beauties. But rather pin up your cards on every board that you find. These are very common in restaurants, community centers, laundromats and etc.
- Leave Behinds – leaving a few cards left behind on a counter at local businesses, or senior centers barber or

beauty shops, and medical offices, including dentists, family medicine, chiropractors, and hospitals. These places are prime territory! Remember to ask if they mind, and tell them how much you appreciate it. You can also leave cards behind with clients. Cards are also great to leave on tables if you are doing seminars.

Since this is a book based on 40+ years of successful sales tips, let's go back to the beginning. When I first started selling, the company provided me with very impressive red, white, and blue embossed cards.

Needless to say, I was proud of them because they were the first business cards I had ever had. But I really learned a serious lesson about using cards in a sales interview. On my first or second solo call to make a sale I encountered "the business card disaster." The prospect listened intently to my presentation and showed some interest. When I used a couple of "canned" closes that did not work. She asked me, "Do you have a business Card?" Can you imagine how excited I was to actually give her one of my pride and joy cards? I whipped out a card and proudly said yes, I do. Here I learned it is important to know how and when to use your card. Timing is important. Because I learned quickly, do not use it in the presentation and let a prospect win. At that point the prospect became totally in control of the meeting. Her comment was, "thank you, I will give you a call when I am ready." What could I do? There was just no response for what she had just said. For a long time, I did not carry cards into an interview, but did the research and found secrets to make the cards work for me.

Yes, business cards are a great inexpensive tool when used correctly. Today in the interview situation when asked for a card I now say, "I will be happy to get you one in a minute" and go right on to the next point in my presentation. This keeps me in control and not the prospect.

Another good use is for referrals. I never send out any correspondence, even birthday cards, that does not contain 3 to 5 business cards. I am sure that lots of the cards are thrown away, but remember the cards are cheap and if only a few are distributed by clients it is a winner. I have found that 2 to 15 new prospects contact us every month and most have need of my service and are eager to schedule an appointment.

How about those fish bowls that offer a free meal or item from a business? These are almost always sponsored by a sales organization. Here we are collecting cards from others which helps with prospecting. The cost again is very low. The item offered is paid for by me, the business will gladly display the "fish bowl" for me because they are getting a sale paid for by me, and maybe a new client for them. This should be collected every month to have a constant supply of lead cards.

I am sure that many of you have read the book "How to Sell Anybody-Anything" by Joe Girad. But did you know he was a high school dropout that became known as the world's greatest car salesman, and a respected author of four successful books on selling

Joe Girard knew that to be successful, **required repeat business and referral business**. That is why he "only sold a Girard" – not cars. He was completely authentic in his pursuit of relationships with his existing customers – and prospects. He cared about what was important to them.

Joe was a very creative marketer. One of the most famous stories of his creative marketing was: He would go to an NFL game. He would sit in the upper deck even though he could afford the more expensive seats in the lower level. When the home team scored and everyone stood to cheer, he would toss his business cards offering a next day discount, to the lower level with the more expensive seats. Yes, marketers work at ways to get their cards in the hands of prospects. Having heard his presentation on sales he said tossing cards did work and he sold cars from this practice.

His sales record of the most cars sold in one year was 1,425 in 1973. His income in 1974 was $189,000.

Here are some additional ways to use your business cards, after you take them out of your desk drawer and dust them off.

1. Be Creative

As we said earlier create different cards with different purposes. One may be used to offer something special with the use of the card. For example: 10% off, a free gift, or a review of their current situation. If you think of a creative way to get your cards in the hands of prospects before your competition, you are out front toward getting sales.

2. Remember the 250 rule.

Everyone you meet generally knows about 250 people to whom they could pass along your card. Just be sure to get cards to them so they can share. How do you get them to share? Simple, just ask the for their help. If they are happy with you, they will be more than happy to pass along your information. It is human nature to tell others about any good deal we received.

3. How About the 1 to 1 Ratio.

This is the easiest ratio you will ever use. It is so simple. If you talk to someone new for one minute, they should have one of your business cards in their hand. Remember first impressions are made very quickly. Think of your conversations like an elevator ride. People get off an elevator quickly, so use the short time of your meeting to get your card in their hands.

Basically, you need to find a way to talk about what you do, and get your business card in their hand within the first minute of the conversation. This takes practice, so go to work on your mini presentation. Here is a good question I have used to complete the 1 to 1 ratio. "I could use your opinion." I have a new business card, "What do you think of it?" If they offer to return it just tell them you have a lot and they are welcome to keep it. With a little planning you too can find a quick catchy saying for 1 to 1.

4. Design a Keeper Card.

What would make a person want and keep your card. Not much. You need to have a card that will spark interest in what you sell. Your card must have a value feature, your card should have a quick summary of what you do. One line summary of what you do is hard to develop, but once you discover the catch phrase that works for you the cards will become an invaluable tool. Remember, do not over clutter your card. Do not try to give to much information. Use only the basic information about you and what you do.

5. OK, they have your card. What now? You will need to inspect the design of your card. Take a look at your card. Would you want to keep it for future reference if not, take a look at the cards you have on file. What made you keep the cards you have kept? If you find cards that are instantly eye catching. Then make sure your card has the same qualities. If it does not have them,it might be time to redesign your card. Basically, I use two cards. One has my name, phone number, email and website. It is plain white and looks very professional, like lawyer or doctor would use. No logo, no advertising, just plain and simple. I use this one when making a mailing that is used just to introduce myself. The letter is definitely a pre-approach item telling them that I will be calling soon. (By the way, the letter is also on very professional stationary that matches the card and envelope.) On a pre-approach letter ALWAYS mail first class. Prospects are busy and many successful business people will not even open "junk mail". For many years my assistant would sort the mail. I told her if it does not have a first-class stamp, do not bring it to me. You would not believe how much time this saved. Remember, you must make everything professional. The second card is used after the prospect has met me. It has my company logo, phone number website, email address and an appointment time on the back side. I also use them in every piece of mail I send to clients so they can give them to friends and family.

6. Business Cards and Parades – Lots of people go to parades. Sometimes candy is thrown along the route. I usuall toss candy suckers with a business card. I punch holes in the card and slide it over the stick. Be sure to toss them to the ground to keep from hitting someone and causing injury. Sometimes, I hire students to walk in a parade and hand out the suckers. Of course, they know to give them to children, but also to hand them to the people who might fit the profile of someone interested in my product line.

Spend Money, Leave Cards – The next time you have lunch or dinner out, notice on or near the counter a box or tray with business cards. Be sure to ask if you might put some cards in the box. If there is not a place to leave cards, simply ask if you could leave a few (4 or 5) on the counter.

Cold Calls and Cards – When making a cold call the process should reverse. I have found that left cards very seldom make it to the desk of the decision maker. When on the initial "hot Knock", better than cold call, your objective is to get the information or card of the person in charge. Once you get that person's card you can make a good old fashioned snail mail letter to introduce yourself and let them know that you will be calling soon. It is so much easier when you know who to contact. It is usually a waste of time just leaving a card like every other sales person has done.

Remember cards in a drawer only attract dust, not appointments!

Time Management

Sink or swim is greatly related to how an individual manages their time. Time is a limited quantity and without proper management it can disappear right before your eyes. You will not realize it's importance until it is too late.

People who become sales failures are most often not able to control their time. Studies have shown that 95% of people do not have the ability to work on their own. This chapter and the following "The APE "will focus on how to best manage time for desired results. To be successful in selling one must be their own supervisor and control their workday. If you are new to selling or an old pro, without proper time scheduling you need to start your self-management program right now.

"Most anything can be fixed with some good ole fashioned time management."

As of this writing, the trend is quickly moving toward working from home. That makes managing your daily schedule even more difficult. Working from home is difficult but add the distractions of daily living, it can become a disaster.

Let's look at some problems and some solutions for working from home.

- **Interruptions** – Family members, yes even the most caring and delightful people in your family can be a distraction for you and they often are not even aware of the situation. Have you ever been in the middle of a project that requires a lot of thought, and a family member comes to you with a request for help? For example, could you open this jar, can you help me for a moment, I want you to look at something, and on and on. How about being on a conference call and the dog starts barking. Ever happen to you? Here is another typical interruption, the doorbell rings at the most inappropriate time. Something simple like a delivery, sales call, or any noise inside or outside of your work area can immediately distract us from important projects. To solve the interruptions problem, it is best to have your work area away from others and the normal activities of family living. The area should have a door and make it known that when that door is closed you are working and not to be disturbed. When I am working my wife usually goes to our sunroom and reads, facetimes, or makes calls so she does not interrupt my working. I am so appreciative of these jesters that helps me more than she will ever know. To succeed in working at home you must minimize or eliminate interruptions.

- **Errands –** it is so easy to find things to do that don't involve your workday. Have you ever been involved in a project and the phone rings? The caller wants you to do something, like pick up the kids from school, go to the bank, pick up the cleaning, get prescriptions, and on and on. It is so easy, (I speak from personal experience) to just get up and do the errand and say to myself I will start working again as I get back. How many times have you done this and in the end, too much time passed, and you never returned to work that day? The solution to this is discipline. You must set your work schedule and STICK TO IT! If you were at a work site and had specific hours, you could not stop for errands. So why do it at home? Tell you family members that you are on the job and cannot be doing anything not related to your work. Tell them don't ask for anything unless it is an emergency. At first, they may think you are rude and non-caring. They will soon learn the importance of your valuable time in the office.

- **Chores** – The weather forecast is for rain later today, and the lawn is five inches high and really needs to be cut. Okay, let's hurry and mow before the rain. Then we can get the business work done. Great idea, but the lawn mower breaks down and you end up spending the rest of the afternoon at the repair shop. "There goes another rubber tree plant" to quote Frank Sinatra. There are so many things calling for your attention. Work can easily go by the wayside in a hurry. Remember there will always be something that needs to be done right now. But work must come first. By the way, back to the lawn mowing story. If you make $200 an hour or more for your work. Why in the world would you use an hour to mow a lawn, when you could contract a mowing service to do it for around $35? Do the math don't ever waste your valuable time.

- **Focus** – most salespeople tend to have a short attention span. It is easy to drift away into thoughts not related to productivity. If you are reading material that will help you in your work keep a highlighter handy. You purchased the educational material, and it is for your use. Marking in a book or making notes is your privilege since you own the material, and it is your property to use as needed. But my point is, know your focus time and relate to it. If you are working, you need to know how long you can focus and stick to that time. Then take a personal break. To me focusing means that I must be result-oriented. The time a project takes is irrelevant if we get our desired results. Always stay focused.

- **Conference Calls and Webinars** – Today more and more meetings, training sessions, and discussions are being held via the internet. This is a great way to communicate while working from home. However, there are problems associated with this technology like any other work from home. Does this sound familiar? There is a stack of paperwork on your desk and a long list of received emails in front of you. This distraction can lead to missing important information from the call or webinar. It is so easy to be distracted from those attention calling items on your desk. This past winter I was on a webinar with an individual who left his video on while attending the same webinar. He managed to go for coffee, leave to get a breakfast roll and take 3 phone calls before the session ended. I just wonder what he gained from his "attendance"? Remember if you take the time to join a webinar or call, pay attention so you will not miss something very important. My advice is, before the session clear your desk and turn off the cell phone. Try to avoid any distractions that might take your mind away from something you really want to learn. Don't waste your investment. The paperwork, phone calls, and emails can wait.

My philosophy has been to always work first, play later. How about this? Try getting your sales goals finished by Wednesday of each week. Then take off a couple of days to reward yourself. If you don't have your work done by Wednesday work Thursday and the same goes for Friday or even Saturday. During my entire tenure in sales, I worked very few Fridays. Why? Because I used the idea of working early and playing later. This is a simple principle of good time management. Don't be like the salesperson who fails by reversing this method of being your own supervisor.
#1 Work Hard
#2 Play Hard
Only in that order. Then 4-day weekends are always great.
Now let's move to my successful method of proper time management in the next chapter entitled "The APE"

The APE

Of all the sales ideas I have used, this is one I developed while managing a group of twelve salespeople. The APE is a great management tool for making sure sales reps are doing the necessary work to achieve their goals. After working with salespeople and the APE I found that as an individual it also could improve my personal sales and individual habits. Yes, even today I use this simple form to help me succeed. You should really consider making your own APE every week. Once it starts to work for you, don't stop using it just because it works.

Personally, I believe that the APE is the most significant idea in this book. There are many facets of selling, but the APE is the foundation.

Let's start at the beginning with a detailed discussion of how to make and use an APE.

As a manager, I was required by my company to hold a weekly "sales meeting" with my staff. At least that is what the company called these Monday morning disasters. I soon learned that these sessions were merely B. S. conferences. Let me explain.

A weekly sales meeting simply is an opportunity for the
representative to sell the manager by inadvertently or purposefully lying to that manager. By the way, this is usually the best sale the rep will make all week. Here is how it goes.

Monday Morning.

The rep or agent comes to the 9:15 A M meeting. The manager is waiting, and the scene is set. After some chitter chatter and friendly conversation the actual synopsis of a failure begins.

The manager asked the salesperson how was last week? Here the "failure" begins, as the rep starts to explain the reasons as to why no sales were made or the goal was not met. The manager, trying to be sympathetic,listens to these reasons, even though he has heard the same from the 8:30 meeting with another rep. The salesperson talks about the long, lonely hours they put in during the previous week. He or she gives all the standard excuses.

- People were just not buying
- The economy is tight
- Prospects just did not have the budget
- He or she was stood up
- Had car trouble
- Made so many calls and could only get one appointment
- Was sick one day
- The kids were sick
- People are waiting for the new model or style.

After hearing these excuses, the manager listens and agrees with the salesperson and answers with the standard management responses.

- This week will be better
- How could I help you
- Do you have any prospects for this week
- Call me if you need anything
- Here are some new leads for you

If you are working for yourself and not for a manager. Here be careful that you do not sell yourself who is also the manager. Simply ask yourself about the reasons why there were no sales last week. Answer honestly and see if you are setting up for failure. You are the rep and manager, so be sure that you are not buying your own excuses.

Week after week this batter continues between agents and managers. After a few weeks the manager must report to his supervisor. And guess what? The same scenario continues. The manager starts to make excuses for the failure just as the people who report to him or her, had made in the weeks before.

Now we begin to see the same thing all over again. The manager begins to sell the supervisor. He either wins or the supervisor wins. Over time either the manager or the representative will be dismissed as a failure.

I think failure is involved with the "sales meeting" process. Using these methods, we are simply stating problems with no idea of how to improve them. Same O same O. As Coach Mike Krzyzewski of Duke University said, "You can't complain about the results you didn't get from the hard work you didn't do."

So how do we make all this "hard work" pay off? I have never known how an excuse could improve any situation. Yes, I know some tragedy like a death in a family is a reason for no production. But that is not an excuse but it is a valid reason. Make sure you can identify excuses from valid reasons. If you take your own excuse or your manager takes your excuse it is only kicking the can farther down the road. Eventually, someone must pay the piper. So let's not focus on the excuses, which we cannot manage, but rather focus on how to honestly find our solution to the problem.

	M	T	W	T	F
A	_____	_____	_____	_____	_____
P	_____	_____	_____	_____	_____
E					

Now that you have seen the APE, how do you use it?

First of all. Let's change the name "Sales Meeting" to "Positive Production Planning" (PPP). Now we can use the time we have been wasting in the so-called sales meetings and use it to make improvements for the individual not to just a time to hear excuses.

Here is how it goes.

Now we change failure to success. Each week you need to develop your APE. I personally like to complete my weekly APE on the weekend, so I am prepared for the upcoming week. If you are in management and working with people and their planning, it is good to meet with them at the beginning of the week or possibly at the end of the week. Never in the middle of the week.

If you are an individual, you can develop your personal plan in the same manner.

For the first meeting or your individual PPP session you need to start filling in the blanks on the APE.

Where do we start? **Always** start with the personal things you want to do during the upcoming week. In the APE bracket, list what you want to do for personal time before scheduling your work hours. For example, Monday Afternoon there is a PTA meeting, Wednesday evening you are having dinner with friends, Thursday morning you play golf or bowl in a league, Friday night is dinner out, Saturday is home chores, kids ball games and family movie night. And don't forget your Sunday church service or any other personal activity.

The personal items outside your work schedule should always be the first things you list on your APE each week. And of course, they will be different each week.

Now let's see what our partially completed sample APE looks like.

M	T	W	T	F
A _____	_____	_____	Golf	Paperwork and PPP For next week
lunch	lunch	lunch	lunch	lunch
P PTA Meet1PM _____	_____	_____	_____	_____
E		Dinner out		Family Movie Night

How does this promote more sales opportunities? Let's look at the A, P, and E of the APE.

If the A of the APE last from 9:00 Am to Noon each day you have six available times for appointments during the mornings, even after personal items are already scheduled.

Continuing, if the P of the APE is from 1:00 PM to 5:00 PM each day, you will have another nine opportunities for sales appointments during that week.

Lastly is the E or evenings of the APE. This can be used for appointments or the entertaining of clients. If your profession does not include nighttime sales appointments use evening times for relaxation or ways to improve your knowledge. This still leaves us three more possible times for sales work.

Let's now total up the amount of time we have for production. In a week we have time for 15 appointments. First, we made room for what he or she wanted to do personally while working only nine to five each day. The evening offers an additional three possible sales times, or client entertainment but let's not count these hours as productivity time but use them for personal items.

Focus now, if you will, on the amount of time you can be productive. In our sample we have allocated a total of 18 hours for personal things to do. And get this, we also have a total of 26 hours to devote to our actual work week. Wow, so simple. Without proper planning we have no idea of how much quality time is wasted or used for distractions.

To avoid these distractions, I do my APE on computer and share them with family members, so they know when I need to work and when I want to play.

Finally for the managers who need to improve sales and work with representatives the following should help you with your task. I have a comical story at the end that will show just how this works with salespeople.

The following will be an illustration of a manager and a representative talking after starting the use of the APE. But as an individual, you can develop your personal plan in the same manner, just don't lie to yourself.

When you first start using the APE work with the agent and make sure he or she has a good working knowledge of how to complete the planning. The planning must be completed prior to each week of selling and fun. Remember, be sure and complete the personal items first. As a manager if you don't make time for personal items, the rep will do them anyway and will then lose track of how to manage their sales opportunities.

I believe that working first is the most important part of the week and playing should only come after successful sales. But if you plan properly there will be adequate time for both. As earlier stated, work hard first then play hard. As the song the "Gambler" illustrates with the words "Never count your money while sitting at the table, there'll be time for counting after the dealing is done." So goes sales. When you are playing first and making sales last you are counting your money before the work is done.

A very important part for the manager is to get the representative accustomed to putting prospect's phone numbers on the APE. This is essential for the manager's use in the follow up the next week in the PPP session. Half or more of the time in those sessions should be spent in review of the previous week's APE. Now, how do we control the "falsifying" of the verbal report from what was on the APE? It is so easy. The emphasis is on putting prospect phone numbers on each appointment listed on the APE, and this is not an option. Make the salesperson always include the phone numbers. At first you may have to help them complete the APE in your presence, but your goal is to get them to the point where they will have it completed on arrival at the "PPP". Once you reach that point all you must do is ask to see next week's APE after you have reviewed the previous week's results.

As I said in the beginning of this section, I would share a comical illustration of how the APE does its job. Yes, this is comical, but the sad part is it is a true story.

Upon reviewing an APE with an individual who was struggling with sales for about three weeks. We again discussed results and saw little improvement. I had the following question of the salesperson. I see you had an appointment with Mr. Jones on

Tuesday, how did it go? The sales meeting type of responses and excuses ensued. After listening I simply said let's see if I can help you. (Remember I said phone numbers were required. Here is why.)" I picked up the phone and dialed Mr. Jones. The first time no answer. So, I asked how you got in touch with the prospect. Here came the mumble and fumble response. I then moved to the prospect on Wednesday of the APE. I dialed that prospect and asked that individual the following: "Good morning this is_____ of _____ company. Our representative_____ called on you last week. I am _____'s manager and I just wanted to know if there was any way I could help you with your decision about our product line? When the prospective buyer said "Mr. who came here? I don't remember him." I then thanked him for his time and informed him that if there was ever a need for our services, we would be more than happy to work with him.

TALIK ABOUT A RED FACE. I wish you could have seen the representative's reaction. Of course, we had a follow up private discussion. From then on, the future APEs were accurate and had valid names and numbers. Talk about a turnaround, this person became the office leader in six weeks.

Another use of the APE is to call later without the rep and discuss the prospects needs, again just ask if there is anything you could do in the future. This has often led to more sales for the agent.

If you need to do weekly or daily "ride a-longs" with the salesperson, make sure there is a completed APE with you so there will not be down time from not having enough appointments scheduled.

The APE will work if you faithfully use it. Even after 40+years personal experience it still works for me.

Remember the old saying, "Plan your work and work your plan." My philosophy has been and is, 'WITHOUT A PLAN YOU WILL FAIL."

I feel that lack of organization and planning is the greatest reason for one being on the road to sales failure. Yes, some people do not have the personality for sales. It is hard to juggle all the balls at one time. If you can master the self-discipline to monitor yourself and plan in advance, the road to success becomes more attainable.

For me sales have been a truly rewarding career in more ways than one. I have had the opportunity to help so many individuals. From the time I made a health insurance sale to an older lady and saved her a lot of money, and she looked across the table with tears running down her cheek and said, "Now I will have money to by groceries." Needless to say, we both had tears of joy running down our cheeks. At that moment my commission was not even my thought. My focus was on how to help her. As I said before, take care of your clients and the commissions will take care of themselves.

No, sales are not always positive events. I too have a large "bone yard" of failures along the way. An example of how some nonprofessionals in our field operate is shown by this actual event form my managerial days.

I was training an "experienced agent" who had recently joined our company. On that particular day I was riding along to observe his sales process and to help him learn our objectives and product line. He had scheduled a call with an elderly lady in our town. The presentation was made and the close was upon us. He attempted several of his previously learned closes and none would work. She finally told him that she would not make any decision without first praying about it. This "salesman" immediately jumped up from his seat and said, "me too". He dropped to his knees and asked her to join him in prayer. Afterwards, he did close the sale. When we got to the car he said, 'that's how you can fool an old lady. Yes, he is in the bone yard of failures. As soon as he made the comment about fooling a prospect, I said, "when we get back to the office clean out your desk you are fired."

I gave this last example to remind us of the fact that honesty, planning, and faith must always be a part of your career. I am sure that he will be reminded of that one fine day.

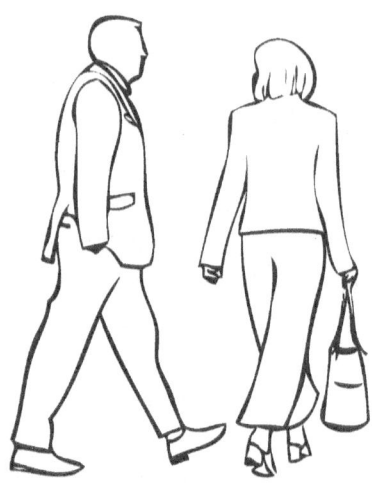

Forget About me. So, I Can Forget About You

During my career I have noticed countless times people are dissatisfied with their service or the lack of service they receive when they are the customers. This is a significant factor in the retention of clients.

I have two friends who sell air conditioning equipment. Although they work for different companies, they both have basically the same products and services. One of them is known to respond when the customer calls with an order. This is his method of staying in contact.

The second spends a portion of his "selling time" making phone calls, sending emails, and taking clients to lunch, a ball game, or just dropping by to make sure everything is doing well. I put selling time in quotes, because I am sure you will agree that these type calls are also selling time. By the way the income for the second representative is three times that of the order taker.

Speaking of order takers, look around. You will see those who are successful and those who "do their job". Not picking on any professions but here are some glaring examples of order takers not salespeople.

- Car Sales – most car salespeople sit around having coffee, reading the paper or just chit chatting while waiting their turn for the next walk in who wants to buy a car. Suggestion, why not use time to be on the phone, addressing thank you cards, sending birthday cards, etc.

- Real Estate Sales – Did you ever see a realtor who puts up a sign in the yard and waits for the call. Marketing is more than just listing and waiting. Enough said.
- Insurance Sales – Have you ever seen more people fail in a profession than insurance agents? For me I have seen more than you could imagine. Most would tell you they were busy, always there on the job. They were active and put in the time but could not make the sales needed. Yeah, very busy, sorting prospect cards, looking up numbers of those to call, sorting more cards, two-hour lunches, sorting more cards, picking up the dry cleaning, children, groceries, and on and on. Sure, they were spinning the wheels, just like going shopping on a stationary bike and not getting anywhere.

These are a few occupations and examples of failure. I am sure you could change the names and put in your occupation and see like people doing the same things in your sales areas.

Here is a good question to ponder. Why do theatres have matinees? The answer is. So, salespeople will have something to do in the afternoons. Don't get caught. Sales can be a lonely life, and no one tells you what to do other than yourself. (More about this in the Chapter on Time Management and the APE).

How much is enough customer contact and how much is too much?

Don't bog down your clients with useless junk mail and insignificant information that they do not care about. Personally, I recommend using a quarterly newsletter about changes in their area of interest. Usually this is by email because it is quicker and more convenient than traditional snail mail. If there is an important product change, such as a recall, price, or any other change I let them know ASAP. Keep them informed but not bored.

An hour or two a month can be spent on not forgetting birthday cards or Christmas cards. This is so important that most salespeople never do it.

I have a card system that really works, before the first of the month I address all my cards at once. Then where the stamp goes on the envelope, I write the number of the date to mail the card. That number will be covered by the stamp. I like to send it four days before the actual birthday, so they get it on or near the actual day.

Several years ago, about ten, I purchased a car from a salesperson I had never met. Would you believe that to this date I still get a birthday card and an email from him? When car shopping his dealership is my first stop because he stays in contact.

Remember the song "Little Things Mean a Lot" it can be the anthem for successful, caring salespeople.

One thing we in sales need to do is not have any down time. If you have a couple of hours that are not filled with appointments or calling time, why not just call some of your existing clients with a short hello and simply ask how they are doing. My call usually starts with, "I was thinking about you today and thought I would give you a call". Sometimes they need an answer or an appointment. Sometimes nothing, however, they are always satisfied with "my check on you" call. These calls do not have to be frequent but keep track of who you have called so you are not becoming a pest by calling the same client repeatedly.

Other ways to stay in contact is the informal drop by just to say Hi. Keep this short and very friendly. Just ask if there is anything you can do for them. If it is not a conflict with your company rules leave them a token of your appreciation. I really like quality pens with my information. Don't use those cheap drops everywhere, plastic pens. Give them a good pen and they will be appreciative and use it. And by the way, the person who greets you and the assistant of the client also like nice pens and will remember you. It makes it a lot easier to get in to see you client next time.

While we are talking about pens and other contact items use only what works. We Midwesterners often say, "You need to dance with the one what brung you". If you find an item that helps clients remember you stay with it. For me quality metal ball point pens have worked very well. You may not believe this, but I have clients that actually call me when they need a new one. When on appointments from referrals prospects often tell me that their friend who referred me told them about my nice pens. You should be known for quality in everything you do.

Also, I do use the low-cost plastic pens at times. Think about contacts made by leaving a handful inexpensive pens at the checkout area in restaurants or any place you visit and spend money. Servers are always looking for pens for taking orders. Tell them to remind you when they have "given" out all their pens. Yes, customers do keep those pens. Keep them in the hands of people who give them out. I also leave cups of pens at senior centers or facilities my clients visit. I drop by and make contact about every month to restock and stay in contact with the director.

Another contact item that has been super successful are magnetic calendars. I purchase a yearlong calendar that fits into a regular #10 envelope. If you are in home sales these magnet calendars always end up on the fridge. In an office they end in the break room or on a file cabinet. The good news is they are used and keep my name in front of clients. Also, I use the ones that fit in a #10 envelope because every client I have gets one every year in January. Postage is expensive, so buy a year's supply before any price increase.

Today, another method of contact is social media. I did not realize how fast information travels on social media outlets. Many times, satisfied clients or friends will repost your information. Good contact little cost.

Many people have asked me what about newspaper and direct mail. I leave that for my competitors. After many tries of trying to make contacts through media nothing seemed to work. How much junk mail do you get? I get enough that I don't even look at it. Lots of ads and mail pieces are just that, Ads. Remember, I said "No first Class Stamp = round file. My late father-in-law was a treasure. I visited him one Sunday and noticed two stacks of the Sunday paper on the floor. I asked him why was the newspaper in two stacks. One is for reading, the other for the dog. Can you guess what was used for the dog? You're correct the ads.

Be sure to focus on the Referral system I use in a later chapter.

Keep singing the song "Little Things Mean A Lot"

Boy Scouts are Prepared

Early in life we learned the boy scout motto was "be prepared". You should be prepared too. It is impossible to be ready for every situation, every day but we should go into the sales meeting as prepared as possible. I have found a few questions that are important to clients. As you know, I am not a canned presentation or answer guy, but I like to prepare for what may come up. Listed below are some questions from clients that have repeatedly occurred over my career. Do not memorize the responses below but understand what you need in order to answer them.

1 How has this program or product worked for others?

Your goal here is to share a story or stories about highly successful results your clients have received from your service. Here you should build your credibility and make them want to do business with you.

2. What type of products or services do you offer?

Here the question is really what kind of work do you really do? If for some reason I did not tell them that I specialize in the area we are discussing. Here I like to use a four-color biographical flyer about me and what services I provide. In the flyer I discuss my education, professional designations and the strength of my business. Testimonials are also good for the back side of the flyer.

This is not a time to be modest. If you've got it flaunt it. Let them know you are successful.

3. How often do you follow-up with your clients?

When you are talking with your clients you must be honest about this topic. Do not over state your contacting abilities. To answer this, I suggest you use something like I do. My clients are told that I will contact them at least every year to make sure they are up to date and have the best available program. I also say that I will contact them with cards, email, mail, and in person. I also make sure they know that they are always welcome to contact me by phone, email, letter or from my website. DO RETURN THE CALLS!

4. I have had the same representative and company for years.

Here you really need to learn if they are happy with their service, products, and company. If they are happy you have to be really careful, and you do not want to ever disparage any competitor. This is a good place to stress your service and why you would be the better contact for service. Today, customer service has become a dinosaur. People forget that long term positive service keeps the client. So many prospects see a sales person only at the time of sale. If they are not happy where they are, it is a positive place for you to be. It is a buying signal. Here your job is to close the sale. Explain your methods of completing the paperwork, purchase order, or order form. Usually if a prospect tells you they are unhappy with their current situation, take action. Close on a point like your service, product line, or your availability. Let them know that you will be working for their best interest at all times. Be available.

5. Do you know of any other professional people that will provide the service like you do?

I have networked many years with financial advisors, attorneys, and Certified Public Accounts. The people I recommend are people that I trust. If I encounter any person that does not keep my standards, I immediately terminate any relationship with them. Do not partner with anyone you have not thoroughly investigated. Over time I have also learned that property and casualty insurance agents often, can help with your service recommendations. However, be careful, because a dent in a fender can really deflate your credibility if it is not handled properly. Make sure the P and C agency is reputable and highly rated. My thoughts are that you only network with people you yourself use or would use. If they have a current advisor, but want to work with you, they will likely need to give up the relationship and network that advisor may offer if he networks. Make sure you can provide support for whatever they may need to insure that the transition is easy. Remember, quality networking increases your reputation and the reputations. of your network.

Here is a thought, if you are selling a service-related item or intangible product why not have joint informational sessions with your clients, the network's clients, and prospects. This reciprocal working together is true networking.

6. Your place or mine?

Depending on the type of sale you are making it may be in your office, their office, in their home or another location. So, let's look at each of the above.

Many times, if you can meet in your office, it is the best location. What you need is there. For example, your computer, product supplies, your samples, and you are close to anything you might need. And another thing is that you are more in control.

If your location is not suitable or you only make field sales be prepared. By that I mean you need have a well-organized sales kit. This can be a file box or something larger that you keep in your trunk. It should have an adequate supply of brochures, forms, samples, extra pens, and any other common supply item you use in sales presentations.

In home selling is often a very relaxed atmosphere. People are in their comfort zone and do not feel threatened. Be aware of signs that indicates their interest. Don't be obvious, like commenting on a family picture. If you use a picture pick out one point and ask about that specific item. This can start the conversation. Should you be working with a retired person a good starting point is to ask about their job. That has been a major part of their lives for many years, and after retirement that main focus is no longer talked about, and they are ready to discuss the past. As with each of the other locations for selling make sure you will have everything you will need. Just like the scout Always Be Prepared.

7. How do you get paid?

The last item we will cover is the personal aspect of your sales. People usually are not nosy, but they often want to know if they will have to pay you. Here be honest, if you are paid a commission tell them that is how you are paid. Should they want to know how much you will make, it is your call. If tell them and they think this is a lot of compensation explain that is why you can give such good service to every client.

These are not all the things for which you will need to be prepared but it is a good start. Selling is ever changing, and the questions are becoming more complex in nature. Be flexible and prepare for the changing times.

Many times, we as salespeople, tend to think that questions are objections. Most of the time the questions are far from being an objection, rather they are signs of interest in you or your product. When you get a question be prepared to answer it openly and honestly. Remember, a good question can be a buying signal. This is also a good time to possibly ask a question of your own that might indicate they are ready to buy. A simple indirect trial close can often produce the desired results.

The Age-Old Question: Tangible or Intangible?

The chicken or the egg? I know you have heard this question many times and it still remains a quandary for many people. There is another question that likewise has caused discussions and different feelings for a long, long time. "Which is easier to sell, a tangible item or an intangible product?"

There are as many responses and opinions about this as there are salespeople in the world. I too, do not have the answer, but can assure you that there is a better mouse trap. Don't worry and get to thinking that the grass is greener on the other side. Thinking that one is better than the other will only result in frustration and most likely failure.

What is the better mouse trap? Concept selling.

In order to get his point across to people who mostly could not read or write, Jesus used concepts. These were called parables. They were ideas and stories that were easy for His followers to understand what He was saying. You too must have concepts whether you are selling a tangible or an intangible. After 2000 years of story concepts it is still sale. I am not calling Jesus just a salesman. He was much more than that. He influenced more people and understood the human psyche completely. Use His example in your life and your work.

First, let's look at selling a tangible item.

People new in the selling profession are often told "Sell the sizzle not the steak." But when I am hungry for a steak, I want a steak. That's not really true. Yes, I order a steak but why? I am imagining the great taste and satisfaction of the steak. Sounds like sizzle to me.

As a tangible item we must have a concept about the item. Let's look at why a person wants jewelry or new clothes. Is it for warmth, absolute need, for more in the box or closet, or to impress others?

I choose all the above. Starting with clothing. If it is for warmth, I conceptually illustrate the winter and its bone chilling effects, not the quality or color of the clothing.

If it is an item, we truly need our concept to illustrate how this item can fulfill that need and make life better for them. An example here is that this tangible item will ease a workload and allow more time for them to enjoy what they really want to do. If it is an automobile sell the concept of that vacation trip, driving home in a new car, the new car smell, the comfort of new technology, or how it will impress those around them.

Be it a product or a service having a concept is real. People usually have an emotional experience when buying. It might be called a hot button or a trigger, but they are more likely to buy an idea than the actual item.

Turning to intangibles it is absolute that the concept is what they will buy. How many people really want an insurance policy, a service contract, lawn maintenance, or investment product. You can't hold it, you can't eat it, can't wear it or sleep in it. But there is a need for these items and other intangibles in our lives. How do we get them to make the purchase? Simple, have a concept or story that really illustrates what the intangible can really do. Look at an insurance policy. Did you ever meet someone who just wanted to buy insurance? I never did. In the case of an employer the insurance is not what they want but rather something that will improve the bottom line. Product details are usually not as important as the benefits to the company. Yes, you must explain those benefits, but things like retaining quality employees, cutting cost, simplification for administrative employees, and service that will be provided are really the concepts they want to know. Many times, we focus far too much on the products than the actual benefits.

Since most of my career was either in training or selling of insurance I can really relate to the conceptual method of selling. Let me illustrate.

When universal life insurance entered the world of intangibles most salespeople rushed to the appointments on their APE with a wonderful computer printout. Boy were these impressive to the agent, but totally confusing to the prospect. Columns of numbers, statistics, and obscure facts do not sell. Personally, I never try to sell in this manner. I never went to the product illustration until I have completed my concept of what it can do, why it is needed, and what it will do for them in the future. Most of the time Universal Life was being sold with the prospect being shown charts and graphs comparing how much better the return of money on the illustration is with the new product than the older style whole life. These sales usually did not last, because the agent forgot the concept of why they wanted to purchase it and what it would do for the employee or family. The concept of the benefits are always more important than facts and figures.

I have a friend who is a very analytical lawyer. If you ask him for the time, he will first tell you about the functionality of his watch, how it was built and how accurate it is. You simply ask for the time, not how to build a watch. He is a great friend, but he gives so many facts before answering a basic question.

Remember it is not how the car is built, but rather what it can do for me.

With an intangible, how can the prospect solve a problem before he knows there is a problem? It is imperative that the actual problem or situation be created long before you move to the solution. The client must see that your product or service will solve the problem of which he was previously unaware.

In the investment area I have had many advisors show me a product that will generate future income when most needed.

For me I want to know the basics of the product, but my image of retiring to the sunny South, traveling, or having enough money to survive is my deciding factor. Retirement is scary because the income we have grown accustomed to is suddenly not there anymore. My being a greeter in a store or seeing the picture of my wife having to work as a waitress or cashier in advanced years is quite frightening. When talking to a financial advisor these thoughts are running through my mind. Definitely not just the facts, which are important, but the fear of a possible dismal result is my concern. Here the concept is to paint a positive future because of what the figures will do and show.

I know many of you are saying it is so much easier to sell a tangible product than it is to sell an intangible. Just remember, that in either case, the conceptual method of selling is what gets the results.

Protecting the family, renewing our ride, buying food, purchasing jewelry, clothes, or personal items are ALL based on our emotions rather than the actual need.

I think one of the ugliest items in my home is the furnace. If I needed to purchase on the glamour of the product, it would never enter my domain. But when the temperature is near freezing that ugly furnace is the most beautiful product I own. The concept of the need for warmth in winter is hard to deny even if currently it's ninety degrees.

Finally, plant the seeds of ideas in the garden of the prospects mind. Then watch it grow and produce your needed sales.

41 Ways to Lose Your Lovers. (clients)

If you do the following 41 actions, you can say goodbye to your lovers (sales) because someone else will be there to take away your business.

1. Forget to be a first-class listener during and after the sale.
2. Always delay the answering of phone calls and emails.
3. Be the grasshopper not the ant. Don't plan and prepare.
4. Make the client feel unimportant and not unique.
5. Keep from giving value they can't find elsewhere.
6. In no way impact people in a positive manner.
7. Chase the money not the building of clients,
8. Make a positive result for yourself not the client.
9. Forget about it. Eliminate your follow up with clients.
10. Stop reading. Don't strengthen your mind.
11. Be an island, work only by yourself.
12. Talk more, listen less.
13. Chase more than one rabbit at a time.
14. Never make a cold call. It is below your dignity.
15. Don't always have a positive attitude.
16. Forget birthdays and significant events for cards.
17. Associate with negative people.
18. Make everything about you and your valuable time.
19. Never ask for help from someone else.
20. Don't ask for referrals after every sale.
21. Be a dry sponge. Never soak up new knowledge.

22. Always eliminate motivation and commitment.
23. Focus only on commission.
24. Become a know it all.
25. Never say I don't know but I will get the answer.
26. Do not network.
27. Why help new salespeople? You can't learn from them.
28. Never learn from any person you meet.
29. Do not participate in constant prospecting.
30. Forget your focus is on helping others.
31. Remember just one bad habit will not affect sales.
32. Your close should not be all about them.
33. You must please everyone no matter the cost.
34. Set limits on your abilities.
35. Forget motivation.
36. Be sure not to educate your clients.
37. Concentrate on things of a negative nature.
38. Do not become an expert in your field.
39. Never get close to your clients
40. Exaggerate what clients expect of you.
41. Never plan your upcoming week. (APE)

I know these are negatives in the 41 reasons, but as you read them again ask yourself, "How many of these mistakes am I making? You need to turn these around and make a habit of doing the positive not these negatives. Incorporate into your daily routine the positive solutions for each of the forty-one points listed here.

In summary, sales do not come in a perfect world. Sales come from problems. It is important for you to make prospects aware of their problem, even if they are not aware of the existence of that problem in the beginning. We as salespersons need to participate in your prospect's world and truly provide solutions to improve their happiness or quality of life.

Earlier in my career I had a wonderful manager that understood me as well as the conceptual sales method. One of the many significant "sales gems" and possibly the greatest words of wisdom things Bob A. said:

"TAKE CARE OF THE CLIENT AND COMMISSIONS WILL TAKE CARE OF THEMSELVES.

Don't ever let anyone tell you that you are just a salesperson. You are truly in a distinct profession. Through your efforts people will be more satisfied, happier, and better because what they receive from you, a truly professional, honest salesperson that cares about them.

Nothing ever happens until someone sells something!

Remember God gave us ten commandments to live by. In addition to those, here are some commandments to sell by.

- Always be honest.
- Put your client first.
- Give your profession quality workmanship.
- Be known as a person of good character
- Believe in your product or service.
- Look professional.
- Live a clean life.
- Make your own successes, don't envy other's successes.
- Plan well.
- Keep things simple and explain well.

Happy learning

Let's Have a Free Meal

At the time of this writing there is a trend for salespeople to offer dinner seminars to attract clients. This is a rather expensive way to talk with groups of people at one time, but for many it must be working. If you are interested in selling through seminars let us look at what is involved.

First, it will take a lot of your time, but it can be quite fruitful if done properly. There are companies that will print your invitations, mail them for you and get you the responses. Of course, this is at a cost, but it does simplify the process, and allows you to continue with your regular sales activities. Even when using this service, you will have other things that must be done.

Second, you will have to find a place to hold the event. Remember, I said always use quality in everything you do. That really holds true here. Find a facility that provides the same quality you present at other times. Make sure there is appropriate lighting, privacy, accessibility, cleanliness, handicapped accessibility, and adequate parking. It must be easy on all counts to attract people.

Third, it will be necessary to design your presentation.

- Are you going to use power point.? If so, make a quality program, possibly designed by a professional.
- Are you going to use a white board? This being your plan you need to make sure one is available and is large enough for all to see. Have new markers so you don't run out in the middle of your presentation. Remember the markers leave

lots of dust and can easily be transferred to your face. If you don't believe me, watch coaches who use them on the sidelines and see how dirty their face gets

- Are you going to have one on one contacts? Using this step will require other people attending to help you with these discussions.
- Are you planning on making sales at the event? If so, you will most likely need people for that phase also. If you do have people assisting, have them sit at tables with the prospects not with other salespeople or workers they know.
- Are you using signs? It is important that one provides adequate signage to direct the attendees to the proper location.
- What type of seating? Are you using classroom set up, round tables, or square tables? If you use classroom do not use a full meal agenda. Round tables allow more to fit in the room, but some people will not be able to see the presentation without moving. Table arrangements with all facing your preferred direction seem to work best.

I mentioned above the concept of possibly selling at the meeting. This is not my recommendation. As you know I like long term relationships and it is hard to make lasting clients at a quick meeting and fast sale. Take your time to chat and get leads. Then give a professional presentation one on one, at a later date.

Meal seminars can be productive. But you must know how many sales need to be made from the meeting. Know your cost per meal and know how many dollars must come in from that meeting. Cost must always be less than return.

I titled this chapter Lets Have a Free Meal, because every seminar has those that only come for the meal. Keep this in mind when doing meal seminars. Cost versus sales must govern the type of seminar you are using.

How about seminars that don't require meals? Is it possible to hold group meetings for your clients and staff at their office or place of business? Here you can emphasize the quality of your product or service. This way you will get more people to have positive input about you and your products. Light refreshments often work in this type of scenario. Your client may need training for his personnel to implement your products. Volunteer to come and provide this training at no cost. Again, you will gain more influence over people who will have input in the future.

My original education was based on education, sociology, and math and science. With this educational background and 12 years of teaching at all levels elementary, junior high and college. This background seemed to create a natural tendency to work with prospects as if were simply educating someone. For me the basis of selling is to provide the information necessary before asking someone to decide on purchasing. An informed buyer is more likely to become a long-lasting client over one that has not ben educated. Therefore, let's move on to having educational seminars.

Exactly what is an educational seminar? This is a presentation where you are establishing a rapport with the prospect or prospects. These can even be one on one meetings or can involve a small group. When I first started doing educational seminars, some with meals, I was so excited to have 30 to 50 attendees. Soon I learned that that is too many people. Smaller more concise groups lead to better results. My option is less than 20 per seminar usually is an easier number with whom to work. Even if you only have two people attend the results can be fine. Just remember cost versus income. If it takes more than one or two sales to recoup your investment, your costs are probably too high.

Educational seminars create a way to establish your credibility and gain new prospects. But the question is, " How do you host one?"

I first want to start with the "why" and the difference between educational and sales seminars. Then, I'll cover some tips based on what I've learned from doing educational seminars.

Why hold an educational seminar?

Your event gives prospects the chance to **build their comfort level and trust** as they learn the ins and outs of your product or service. An educational seminar is basically a prolonged warm-up in the sales process. But instead of small talk, you're providing education which causes your prospects to be much more comfortable with you, and they're starting to build up more trust.

Finally, you establish your reputation of credibility in your relationships, community, and that of being an expert in your field when you hold educational events. Everyone wants to do business with someone who's respected and an expert in their field.

Educational vs. Sales Seminars.

An educational seminar is **completely educational** – no marketing or sales activities are going on. You're not talking about any specifics of what you are selling, and you're not handing out any promotional or marketing materials. Finally, during an educational seminar you are definitely **not selling anyone anything**.

A sales seminar is quite the opposite – you are presenting a company's specific product or service. This involves things such as a contract, application, credit application, or enrollment in your offering?

Your goal is to complete the sale, or at least start the process. This is the main difference between educational and sales seminars. More time is usually spent attempting close the sale than on education. I am sure by now you know that my preference is educational because it gives me a chance to gain clients over just a sale. For me an educational offering is the perfect way to introduce myself and give a view of my product or service. And now the tips:

1. It is important to review the company's rules to ensure that you are saying what the management and the legal department wants you to say. If you do not represent a company and use only your own materials use common sense. Make sure what you present is factual and true. You also need to know if the company allows hand out gifts

and if they do what can they provide. Personally, I only use my own personal small trinket, advertising materials. Why? Because I am here to sell **me** and my expertise, not a product or company.

2. The marketing of your seminar should be designed to steer or attempt to steer the prospect toward your credibility and product or service, and to get appointments at a future date to make the sale. Do not get unmotivated, disoriented, or concerned if you are losing some who will not give you an appointment. Remember cost vs. results. One good client is better than a few shoppers.

3. You need to know when to have a seminar. The general rule of thumb is to choose Tuesdays, Wednesdays, or Thursdays. We want to choose a day and time that's friendly to them and works with their schedule. Typically, Mondays and Fridays are a bit sluggish for workers – they're either tired on a Monday or are ready for the weekend by Friday. When scheduling your meetings find a time that works best for you and your prospects.

4. Pay attention to holidays. They can be a nightmare. If you are planning a seminar on a specific date, be sure it is not around or on a holiday. We learned the hard way on this one – if you always hold the seminar on the first Tuesday of every month. For example, we recently, held a seminar that landed on the day after Memorial Day, and it was our worst turnout yet. If you're planning out your dates for the year, **pay attention to the holidays and try to avoid them!** Many people are traveling or don't want to put too many things on their calendar around a holiday. For the best turnout, either move your seminar to the other end of the week or go for the following week.

5. PowerPoint presentations really help. If you are using a PowerPoint presentation don't over think your presentation slides. They should be as simple as can be and still get your point across. Make an outline of what you want the client to understand or learn and then develop your slides

accordingly. By the way, if you have trouble with your presentation slides ask your child or grandchild, I am sure they can help. Actually, a professional can really help with your development.

6. Establish a no-pressure atmosphere. It is best that at the beginning you relax your clients at an educational seminar. I use the following when I start or early in the beginning. "I see some of you ladies brought your purses, and I hope you gentlemen did not bring your wallets. You will not need them this evening because this is an informational meeting only. No one will try to sell you anything here." I let them know that they will not have to provide any information such as your name, phone number, address, or any other personal information. Let them know that if they want more information, you will be happy to meet with them afterward, but they will have to reach out for an appointment. Let them know that you will not call them, they will have to call you to set a time to visit. It goes against what you think you should do because you have this great audience, and you want to capitalize on it. But I think this is the **best way to ensure your audience has open ears** to your presentation. You do not want anyone to feel like you're just trying to sell them something the whole time.

7. No Specifics. Do not get into specific items in your presentation. At times there will be someone in your group that has had a bad experience with what you are presenting. I simply inform them that this is a general presentation and if anyone has a unique question, they can set up a one-on-one appointment with me. I do hand out business cards at the end of the meeting. (Remember, business cards are cheap.)

8. Meals or Snacks? I don't like providing meals, because they might get this lingering pressure to buy something at the end of the presentation. I don't want my attendees to feel that way at all – I want to keep that no-pressure atmosphere, so I avoid meals and instead have light

snacks and refreshments. And light snacks give me more time for my presentation.

9. Shoot for less than 20 attendees. When I am inviting people to a seminar, I have a rule. **don't take more than 20 people,** because it is easier to manage a smaller group. If you have more responses have a second seminar. When you have a larger group, everyone freezes up and they're not as comfortable. I honestly feel like some of my best seminars were 5-10 people! Sometimes you cannot control the number. For example, if you are talking to a professional marketing group, a civic club, church group, or any other meeting where you are the featured speaker. However, a small group is NOT a must. A couple of years ago I held a meeting for a group that the president of the organization did the inviting. He told me that there should be 20 to 25 attendees. On the day of the meeting 84 people came. I must have done a good educational presentation because from that meeting, we received 27 sales. Be flexible and take what is given. 20 is ideal but don't shy away from smaller or larger groups if you must.

10. Have someone take photos. It is much easier to promote upcoming events when you have actual pictures of you making a presentation. People can get a visual of what it's like and you do not have to rely on a stock photo. It is also good to have a video that you can insert on social media showing you and part of your presentation. Video seems to be something that really catch people's eye on Facebook.

11. Are you new in sales? It is best to think twice about holding seminars if you are brand new to sales. When you're standing up in front of an audience, **you need some experience** in order to confidently present the material and answer questions. Nothing deflates your credibility faster than getting a question and not knowing the answer. Plus, for newer agents with 0-2 years of experience, it's a lot more difficult to promote your seminar. Established agents with a large client base and a strong connection to

the community can promote in a lot of low-cost ways, but **new agents will have to spend a lot more** to achieve the same result. If you are new it might be good to use a fellow rep in your office, the company trainer, or just observe several seminars before going on your own.

12. Brochure's help. Earlier we talked about selling yourself and nor a product or service. After several years of selling, I printed my first sales brochure. It was designed to promote me and what I do. Some are credibility building and some promote my seminars or appointments. But all promote me. Depending on what you are marketing check out places you frequent and see if you can leave brochures. Years ago, I had brochures that promoted me and getting appointments. I left them in waiting rooms, but I left them inside the magazines people brose while waiting. I put them inside so they were not thrown away at the end of the day but stayed with the magazines that are not frequently changed. You can use business cards or brochures.

13. Share promotional short seminars on Facebook. I have found that Facebook is a great tool for spreading the word about you and what you do. Let everyone on Facebook see just what you do and how to contact you for information about your next seminar. If it is a video, images, a link to your website, or an event page put it on Facebook.

14. Promote your seminar with no cost. Seminar marketing can be very expensive. I have learned that some people spend up to $4000 on seminars and advertising costs for just one session. Wow, that is expensive. (Remember, cost vs. return) In order to promote your seminar in a less expensive manner, use low or no-cost places. A few ideas are:

- Add a seminar page to your website.
- Write a blog post explaining what to expect in your seminars.

- Share your new pages on Facebook and your Google My Business page.
- Write a press release share it with local papers and radio stations. (Lots have a "who is news" area.)
- Add upcoming seminars to your email signature.
- Change the live chat area on your website to specifically call about seminars.
- Call and email existing clients and ask them if they know anyone who would benefit from your upcoming educational seminars.
- Post flyers at local businesses or bulletin boards

15. Always be ready to make presentations to the groups you have already turned into clients. For example, if you sold products that are to be used by several people in the busines. You can offer a seminar for small groups at various times. Keep them effective and short to not waste paid time. Look at your competitors, after the sale how many are willing to return to help their customers.? I will assure that none or not many will give those seminars. It is always good to be a step ahead of the competition.

Seminars do work. Remember the three P's. Planning, Promotion, and Presentation. Each area must be effective and professional. Do not try to take short cuts. Each step of the way on seminar presentations must be completed in great detail.

Get In The Game

I was never much of an athlete, and when I made a team my course of action was to play three positions at once. Sit on the end of the bench, guard the water bottles and tackle anyone who tries to get them.

But when the coach turns to you and says, "Come get in there!" You had better be prepared. Yes, all the hours of practice, weightlifting and getting shape was for this moment in time. If you are not prepared, you will never get into the game.

Sales is like getting the call to go into the game. You will never know just when it will come, but if you have not made the proper preparations, success will become a ghost.

I know the long hours of studying, learning sales skills, practicing presentations, gaining product knowledge, and being in shape for your moment can be exhausting. Don't give up. Sales can be the most lucrative business of which to be a part. Not just financially, but also rewarding mentally.

Stick it out. Selling is a constant learning process. Hang in there and the rewards will come. In the beginning you may feel success is just not there. Don't you believe it. Hard work, perseverance, planning, a positive attitude and preparation will eventually pay off.

I remember the story of a sales rep who said in his first two years he sold everything. His car, his furniture, his house etc. Do not worry, even if early times are hard, doing the right things over time will pay off for you. Never stop improving in your field. I don't know of anything worthwhile that comes without hard work. You can be super successful if you keep trying.

Over the years I have kept a small stuffed toy of "Wylie Coyote" on my desk. Why? Because I consider him to be the best example of a determined to succeed salesperson. Just look at him. He gets knocked down and fails more times than you can count. But one thing about "Wylie" he always gets back up and gives it one more try.

Yes, early in my career I did cold call direct door to door for sales. Talk about hard. Door to door can only be easy for school children selling fund rising items for their school, sports team, or church. That is not hard, but for the salesperson this may be the hardest of all sales activities. If you don't believe me, give it a try and you will learn very quickly just how hard that sales approach can be.

I remember once while doing sales training with a new person, we were making those dreaded door to door calls. It was pouring rain. We were in raincoats and hats going from house to house. Soaked, wet, and cold we had just had three rejections and was ordered off a person's porch for being "so stupid to be out there on such a bad day". I am sure she was right but with all the negatives of that day, one more call and guess what. We made a nice sale, and more this person became one of our finest referral sources. She knew a lot of people and recommended us to many of them. Lots of sales came from; One more call on a miserable day. Never fail to keep on keeping on.

When trying to sell a Cancer Insurance Policy door to door, I just could not get the sales required. My favorite, wise manager suggested that I spend two days with the top cancer salesperson in the company. I did so and found what was missing in my presentation. He was a master at keeping it simple. Upon arriving at the door, he did not say good morning or afternoon. He simply said his name and asked his first question. "Who has your cancer insurance?' They would tell him their health insurance plan. His immediate answer was, "that's your health insurance plan." It does cover most of the costs that a battle with cancer can create.

Question number two," What would you do if you or your family would become the one out of 4 people to contract this disease? Question number three," How would you cover the cost associated with this disease that are not covered by your health plan? You know Cancer is expensive because it lingers. Could I have five minutes of your time to show you how you could prevent the possible loss of all you have worked for.

No, he did not get into every home, but when he did it was almost an automatic sale as he went through the brochure. He persistently worked four days each week and he worked till he made his goal of 5 sales a day. He prepared and practiced till he was no longer on the bench but became a starter. He made a very outstanding living and was always the leader in his area with the company, even though no one ever wants to talk about cancer. He could create the problem then solve it for them.

No, I did not become a great Cancer Insurance salesperson, but I did sell more that enough to meet my quotas and from that learned a lot about successful selling.

If you are doing door to door, may I say God Bless You!

I believe every salesperson should sell with their ears. Yes, the presentation, the product, or quality of the product or service is important. One should always be listening. Don't be so dedicated to one of those three things that you forget to listen. Always have time to answer questions. For me listening is the most important part of the entire sales presentation. In addition to listening, education is equally important. Put this one in your book. Without education the sale will not be made. In sales our job is to educate the prospect to the point they understand our concept. Without which they avoid making the purchase.

It has been said that when the decision is made to buy the prospect has a "moment of insanity" This may be true with some, but I believe we can avoid that insanity moment with proper educational materials and presentations. Lasting clients come from prospects who know enough about the product or service.

Getting in the game is a conclusion to this book of sales ideas. I would like to give you just a few items not in the sales profession but can and will make you a better salesperson as well as a better person overall.

- Keep your faith. Belief in God is an absolute for a successful life.
- Love you family. Family is the second most important part of one's lifetime. Who really cares? Your Family!
- Maintain the six. I have long ago realized that every person needs six people who will come, no matter what. Those six are the ones you will need to carry you away.
- Love your county. At this time, I see more dissention in our country than ever in my lifetime. If you disagree with our leaders that is fine. Use that opportunity to write and work with them for overall improvement.
- Call on the marines. In the preamble to the Marine Corp constitution, it states a must for marines and salespeople. You must have "pride in the outfit and confidence in the leadership."
- Love is a must. Love your neighbor as you love yourself.

Now that I have condensed forty plus years of my life in sales to one short story. I want you to know that I have had a super successful life from staying in the game with love of God, Family, Friends, and a true confidence in my products and confidence in the leadership that helped me achieve a happy and successful life.

Thanks God, Mary Ann, J. R., Lisa, and Kyle

For you the reader I wish you the same happiness and success. May you have a wonderful life filled with unlimited success.

John

www.ingramcontent.com/pod-product-compliance
Lightning Source LLC
Chambersburg PA
CBHW021442210526
45463CB00002B/611